*We dedicate this book to
Arletta, Jan, Joan, Judy, Karen, Marcia, Margaret, and Susie
with loving thanks to our
Monday night Bible study ladies
for giving us the confidence to pursue our dream!*

Acknowledgments

We would like to thank the following people for their ideas, inspiration, and encouragement to undertake the writing of this book.

Our thanks go first of all to our dear friend, Jim Langham. He listened to our stories, put them down on paper, and critiqued the manuscript. His help was invaluable in clarifying the ideas, and we are so grateful.

Thanks also go to my employer, Marc Graber, of Graber Insurance, Inc., who allows me flexible hours, and my fellow employees who graciously support me as I continue to be used of God in ministry.

And of course, I couldn't have written a book of stories without my family. They are my stories and I love them for allowing me to share them with everyone! To my loving husband, Lee; Toby and his lovely wife, Amy; Jeff and his wonderful wife, Tami, and my precious grandchildren, Sidney and Grady; Aaron and his sweet wife, Kathy; I look forward to many more stories at your expense! Thank you!   — W. K. S.

To the ones who give me so much joy, I give you thanks: My dear husband, Amos; Jennifer and the best son-in-law in the world, John; Bob and my wonderful daughter-in-law, Lisa; to the most precious gifts God has given to me, my six grandchildren: Jessica, our angel; Jordan, our gift of love; Jadriana, our creative joy; Ashlie Jo, our beloved; John Dennis, our reminder of love; and precious little Cierra. I say thank you, Lord, for blessings indescribable.
              — N. G. L.

Thank you, readers, for letting us share our stories with you!
Thank you, Lord, for loving us and giving us the stories to tell.
              — Willa K. and Nancy

Table Of Contents

Five Pieces Of Pizza
And
A Can Of Grape Soda

I was a person who, when I was in that time of my life, wanted to cry all the time. I was fifty years old and all I wanted to do was cry. It didn't matter what it was. I mean, people could look at me the wrong way and I wanted to burst out crying.

I remember one Friday night when I came home from work. Friday nights I always work late so we usually have pizza. I came home that evening and I could tell the moment I walked through the door that I was going to start to cry. Sure enough, I opened the door and it was instant tears. All I wanted to do was cry.

I have three sons. They immediately met me at the door and said, "What's wrong? Why are you crying?"

I replied, "I don't know why I'm crying."

My middle son, Jeff, said, "Mom, I just want to say that I invited Tami for pizza tonight. I knew we were having pizza and I knew it wouldn't be a problem for you, at least not normally."

I said, "Oh, it's all right. I'll have it together by then."

However, it just didn't get any better. I thought I would go to my bedroom. There's no hope in stopping. By that time I had been crying about a half hour. You can imagine how bad I looked. What made matters worse was I could hear how they were getting along without me.

Pretty soon my youngest son, Aaron, came in and said, "Mom, I just want you to know that I took care of everything. I have the table set. I ordered the pizza and they'll be coming. It'll be okay."

"Oh, that's wonderful," I sobbed. "I'm so glad that you took care of everything." Inwardly, I was really upset because he could do it without me.

Then my middle son, Jeff, came in and said, "Mom, is there anything I can do for you? I know you're really upset."

"No, I don't know what you can do for me," I cried out. "All I want to do is get out of here, so Tami doesn't see me like this," I replied. Jeff went off to be with his girlfriend.

Finally, my oldest son, Toby, took his turn. He came in and said, "Just tell me what's wrong."

"I don't know what's wrong," I said.

He persisted. "Just tell me what's wrong."

"I don't know what's wrong," I cried even harder.

Finally, in exasperation he said, "I can't believe it. You always say that if we talk about it, it'll be better. Here I am. I'm asking you what's wrong and what are you doing telling me there's nothing wrong."

"I can't talk about it when I don't know what's wrong," I sobbed.

Toby turned and left in disgust.

There they were, all in the kitchen. I could hear them eating the pizza and having a wonderful time. To make things worse, I had been in my room for an hour crying, listening to them getting along without me, and I had yet to see my husband.

Finally, I could hear them cleaning things up, putting things away, and one by one leaving the house. It got very quiet. Quietly, the door of our bedroom opened. There he was, finally my husband, Lee, with the perfect answer. He had a plate with five small pieces of pizza, the kind that are cut in little squares, and a can of grape soda.

"Here," he said. "Eat a little something and you'll feel better."

Now, husbands, do not ever do that to your wives at a time like that because it doesn't help.

"What will Tami think? I worry that she doesn't think I have it all together. Now I know she knows I don't have it all together," I said.

He replied, "Jeff said you wanted to go for a ride, do you want to go now?"

I didn't want to go for a ride. I just wanted everything to be normal. He didn't understand, but I went to the van and we went for a ride. You won't believe the things we talked about.

"Did you see our neighbors' new shrubs?" he said.

8

Then he went on to talk about some things that were happening at work.

I thought to myself, do I care tonight? I mean my whole life is falling apart and we're going to talk about what's happening at work.

I'm thankful to say that after that I went to a doctor. They've got wonderful things these days to help with this kind of need. He gave me a patch to put on my body and it's amazing how my life changed.

Afterthought ... In Psalm 139:17 and 18 God's Word says, "How precious also are Your thoughts to me, O God! How great is the sum of them! If I should count them, they would be more in number than the sand; When I awake, I am still with You."

Even in the morning we can trust that our God is still with us. Though hard times come and we don't understand why, we can trust Him to always be there. He is constantly thinking of us, the number is greater than the number of the sand. In another verse David also tells us, "Where can I go from Your Spirit?" The Lord is always with us. He is always ready to lift us up, to carry us, to hold us up, and to keep us. We can trust Him.

God's Mysterious Ways

If you think it could never happen to you, think twice, because it could. That's the message I got as I entered into a career I never planned on. You see, I'm on the phone a lot; I'm an insurance agent, actually a customer service representative. I try to help take care of your problem before you have to go to somebody else.

I never thought life would be like this. I always thought that I would be home with the children, and I was until they went to school and I went to work. I'm not working because I want to; it's something that happened when I prayed for a job for my husband.

The large company where my husband was working decided to move out of the town, and so we started to pray that God would open up another job. And he did, the Monday after his plant closed down, but it was a job for me, not him.

"Lord, you don't understand," I said. "I prayed for a job for Lee, not me. He's the one that needs a job."

But that's not how God saw it and so here I am, trying to dress like an insurance agent when I have a T-shirt and jeans heart. I'll never forget the first time I realized that I wasn't natural at dressing up like that. I was wearing a black dress and I went to the bathroom. About twenty minutes later I reached in my pocket to get a tissue and I discovered that my pocket was missing. I said to myself, "How does a person lose a pocket in a bathroom?"

Frantically, but without trying to draw attention to myself, I stood up and discovered the problem. The hem of my dress was stuck in the back of my pantyhose!

I looked around to some of the young girls in the office and said, "Did you know that the hem of my dress was in my pantyhose?"

They laughed and replied, "Yes, but it looked so funny we didn't want to say anything."

You might think it could never happen to you, but it could.

I listen to people who have accidents with their cars, but I've looked at it differently since I backed into three cars in the parking lot at the office. Oh, I don't mean I backed into three cars at the same time. I backed into three different cars three different times.

11

The first one was a friend of one of our management people. I told them that I was sorry but they told me not to worry because there wasn't really that much damage. A few days later they brought me a bill for $497. Back then that was quite a bit of money for damage.

On another occasion, I backed up and hit the car of a co-worker. However, she told me that her car was so banged up that she couldn't see which dent was mine.

The third time involved the car of an insurance man that comes to our company to help us out.

"How can I ever tell him that I hit his parked car?" I thought to myself. The first thing I did that time was to go home and take a black and green pill. Now, black and green pills settle you down so you don't have those awful feelings when something goes wrong. I was sure I would be able to handle this now.

I went back to the office and Kirby came in. He looked at me and said, "Well hi, how are you?"

I totally lost it. I burst out crying and said, "I wrecked your car." The black and green pill didn't help me any and I still had to have his car fixed.

One night late when there was no one in the parking lot, I backed right into a pole.

I thought to myself, "I wonder what that was. There's no one in the parking lot. Why, that's a pole."

My husband and I thought we had the problem solved when I purchased a van. I would start backing into the parking spaces so when I would leave I would drive forward. I would be able to see what's in front of me and not hit anything.

That worked for a while until one day when I was in the drugstore parking lot. I started to back up when something didn't seem right. I thought to myself, well, that seemed funny. I backed up and tried it again, and that's when I saw this real little car that I hadn't spotted before.

I got out and this fellow was standing there just looking at me.

"Did I hit you twice?" I said.

"Yes," he replied, "but don't worry about it. There are so many dents on this little car I don't know which ones are yours."

Do we have insurance? Sure we do, but probably only because I work in an insurance office. If you think that it could never happen to you, don't think that because it could.

Afterthought ... All but one of these vehicles were restored to their original design. This is just the way God works in our lives, at the point of salvation, when we turn our life over to Him He restores us, and He makes us new again. Real restoration is not a cover up. It is new from top to bottom. That's the way we are when God touches our lives; we are new creations. II Corinthians 5:17 says, "Therefore, if anyone is in Christ, he is a new creation; old things have passed away; behold, all things have become new."

Also, so many of us are like the one who did not want his car restored because of too many bumps, dents, and scratches. The gift is ours; the price has already been paid, but we refuse and do not accept this glorious gift.

Today is the day; don't delay. Make your choice; accept His gift of healing, forgiveness, and restoration. The price has been paid!

A "Normal" Day

Several years ago I undertook the project of writing down an entire day in my life. I did it because I was going to speak at a mother and daughter banquet and I wanted a "normal" day for my talk. While the day seemed pretty normal, for the most part, writing it down put it in a different perspective than I had imagined when I first took out my pen and note pad.

When I woke up that Saturday morning, I already knew that I was going to have problems. I had a bladder infection, just a little bitty one, but bad enough to make me have to go to the bathroom every few minutes.

I knew that the day was going to be ruined, just absolutely ruined. Here it was, Saturday morning, and I had all of these things I wanted to do, but now I probably wouldn't be able to do them because of "this problem."

The day's activities started with a request from Jeff. He needed cookies to give to Tami and he wanted to know if I would bake them. I consented, but then I started to wonder, "Which Tami?" He was dating a Tami and he had a Sunday school teacher named Tammy.

I finished the cookies and then, naturally, I called the wrong Tami to tell her I had the cookies made.

She said, "I don't understand why you have cookies ready."

"Because I was supposed to have cookies ready for Tami but obviously this is the wrong Tami," I replied.

As it turned out, I was supposed to have gotten them to Tammy, the Sunday school teacher, but I didn't get them to her, so that blew me away.

Next it was time to get my coupons together to go to the grocery store. I love coupons. I love buying things we'll probably never eat just because I have a coupon for them. But think of it, they triple your coupons and you get something for 17 cents. And there you are, eating a meal for 17 cents.

That was like a game for me. In fact, we had a neighbor lady who loved it so much that she used to write her checks out for the amount that she would have paid. When the cashier would give her money back for the coupons, she would put it toward vacations. They would have wonderful vacations from all of the money she would get from coupons alone.

As I was finishing up the coupons, it dawned on me that it was about time for lunch. Since it was just Toby and myself at the time, I decided to make grilled cheese sandwiches. That led to the next problem. Because I was so caught up in working on the coupons, I forgot to check the cheese sandwiches on the stove and they turned black on both sides. Sometimes you can just scrape them off and make them better but I couldn't do that with these. They were completely burned.

I put the burnt sandwiches aside and started some new ones when my neighbor came walking in.

"Oh, this is great, burnt cheese toasties; I love them," she said. I offered it to her and she thought how wonderful it was that she could sit down and enjoy something that I couldn't throw away.

After she left, I went back to my list. I had just finished it when there was a knock on the front door. No one comes to my front door!

There stood a girl, a pretty blonde girl, and she said, "Does Toby Sprunger live here?" I said, "Yes, he does."

"Is he here today?" she said.

I replied, "Yes, he's in the garage. I'll go get him for you."

"Oh, no, I'll just walk out to him," she answered.

As she walked around the house toward the garage, I started playing that game. I ran from window to window trying to figure this out. Who was she? What did she want with Toby? Was he dating her and not telling me? What was she to him?

I thought to myself, "This is not going to be a problem. Lee will come in and tell me who she is. He'll soon catch on and leave them alone and come in."

Of course, he didn't.

Then I thought that maybe I should just go out there myself. But what was I going to do, take out a can of oil and say, "Here I am, what can I do to help?"

I knew that wouldn't work. I knew I had to have some reason to go out there. I knew that the Bible said in Jeremiah that you're supposed to find wives for your sons. I was doing all that I could. Believe me, everyone was a prospect.

Finally, after what seemed like forever, Toby came in.

I rushed to him and said, "Oh, Toby, who was that?"

"Who was who?" he said.

"That girl that was out there," I replied.

"Oh, she was just somebody I know," he stated casually.

"Well, why did she come here?" I asked.

"She just wanted something, nothing important, Mom," he said. I thought, "Well, he's not going to tell me. I'll just wait and Lee will come in the house in a few minutes. He can tell me what was going on."

Sure enough, Lee came in and I said, "Who was that girl?"

He said, "I don't know."

I said, "You're not paying attention."

"What was I supposed to pay attention to?" he answered.

"He's your son, too. That's your job. What's more important in your life?"

"She talked to Toby and Toby talked to her. I don't know what they talked about. I wasn't listening," was his reply.

Finally, I started getting some wisdom about myself. I knew that I wasn't going to find anything out so I left to go to the grocery store. I had just about finished my shopping when I noticed some Cadbury eggs near the checkout. I just couldn't pass them up. They were on sale and so I bought four eggs.

On the ride home that took three minutes I managed to eat one of the eggs knowing no one would see me. When I got home I offered an egg to Lee and I ate another one myself thinking that I could fool myself that I had only had one! However, we all know it shows!

Then I said to Lee, "Where are we going for supper tonight?"

He said, "You want to go out for supper?"

I said, "Yes, I thought we could."

"Well, didn't you just go grocery shopping?" he said.

I said, "Yes, but there's nothing there that I can fix quick for supper."

"I'll bet there is," he said.

That did it and I got out the Bisquick and made some of the worst pancakes I've ever made. They were awful. It was really a quiet meal. It was like I was going to pay him back because he wouldn't take me somewhere to eat.

Once supper was over, I realized that I needed to start getting ready for Sunday school the next day. I admit that was kind of tough because of the way I had just acted, but you can forgive yourself when you're in a hurry and you have a cause.

Finally, it was time to go to bed, but I realized I had one more thing to do, separate the fish in the aquarium. I had not done it before but I didn't see it as a problem. I knew that anybody could separate fish in an aquarium.

Unfortunately, it wasn't that easy. It should have been. You have this net you drop into the water. How can a fish escape from that? Mine did. I went to this side and they swam to the other side. I went to the other side and they swam back to this side. Finally, I gave up and went to bed upset because I couldn't even catch a fish in an aquarium.

As I lay there I thought to myself, "What have I accomplished today? What have I done today that has been important? I couldn't think of one thing — and this was supposed to be my 'normal' day. And yet, what have I done today that's made a difference in anyone's life?"

If you're like me you pray each morning, "God, help me to be an example; help me to be a testimony; help me to be a witness to someone today."

By that time I was thinking to myself, "This is probably about the most depressing thing I have ever done, and I wouldn't have even known if I hadn't chosen to write down the day's notes for that banquet."

Afterthought ... To be motivated for ministry you must be prepared, ready at any time whether it is convenient or inconvenient to proclaim it. A minister of the gospel is a servant who is ready to proclaim the Word of the Lord. Ministry is service.

Just like the farmer knows the appropriate time to get the soil ready, to plant, to be patient, to reap the harvest, so does the servant of God know when the time is ready to share the Word. Having a heart that is open and ready for service to be used by God, that is what God is looking for. Open vessels ready to communicate His love.

II Timothy 2:3-7: "You therefore must endure hardship as a good soldier of Jesus Christ. No one engaged in warfare entangles himself with the affairs of this life, that he may please him who enlisted him as a soldier. And also, if anyone competes in athletics, he is not crowned unless he competes according to the rules. The hardworking farmer must be first to partake of the crops. Consider what I say, and may the Lord give you understanding in all things."

Peanut Butter Pie

How many of you like it when somebody fusses over you? I like to hear really nice things about myself. I don't like to hear the things that I do wrong, but I love to hear people tell me when I do something right. There's a lot of things I don't do right, so when there is something right, I like to hear it.

One day when I was asked to speak to a group of young mothers, I taught them how to make peanut butter pie. You see, I'm not a cook but Nancy is and she taught me how to make the pie. I have a hard time following directions. My mom used to say, "Just go for it, it'll turn out okay." That might have worked for her but it didn't work for me. My things don't always turn out okay.

When Nancy gave me this simple recipe for peanut butter pie, I thought I had something. Mix peanut butter and powdered sugar and put it on the bottom of a graham cracker crust. Make instant vanilla pudding and put that over the top. Put some more peanut butter and powdered sugar over that, and then put Cool Whip on top. Then sprinkle the peanut butter mixture on the Cool Whip and put it in the refrigerator.

When you do this, it makes any sick meal look great. Do you know those times when you have hot dogs and chips and they say, "Is that all?" Try this and they'll say, "We got pie? Yea, we got pie. This is a great meal."

I was teaching young mothers how to do these kinds of things so they could pull off meals when they'd had tough days with their kids. I wanted their families to think that they were really putting meals on to the table with the least amount of work.

One day I got a phone call from a husband who said, "My wife was at your cooking demonstration."

I thought, "Oh, no, what did I say?"

He said, "I want you to know we are really enjoying peanut butter pie. We're having it every other day now!"

After that phone call, I quickly called his wife and told her how to make banana cream pie, which is about the same thing.

I remember one day when I was going to make a banana cream pie for someone whose mother had passed away. I started out by putting bananas in the bottom, but I forgot I was making banana pie and I put peanut butter on the next layer. When I realized what I had done, I put both bananas and peanut butter mixture on the top.

I'll never forget what the family told me later. "That was delicious. It was the first banana and peanut butter pie we had ever had." Just before I arrived the family had been talking about an old Elvis Presley movie their mother had so enjoyed. They talked about the peanut butter pie in the movie and a few moments later there I stood with the peanut butter and banana pie.

You see, the point of all of this is that we all like to hear that we've done a good job. Do you know what? So does God. As important as it is to sing each other's praises here on earth, it's really important to praise our Heavenly Father. He loves to hear how much you love Him.

As we enjoy hearing praise for our earthly gifts, even more so our Heavenly Father loves to hear praise for the gifts that He gives to us. How good God must feel when He hears how much we appreciate what He has done for us.

Afterthought ... In Judges 5:3 even Deborah sings praises to the Lord. "Hear, O kings! Give ear, O princes! I, even I, will sing to the Lord; I will sing praise to the Lord God of Israel." The Song of Deborah was a poem of victory and is one of the oldest examples in biblical literature.

When we sing praise we are testifying to the great love of God for us; and our love to Him.

Time Stood Still

I'll never forget the trip that Nancy and I took to a retreat in California when it seemed like "time stood still." We were already tired when we arrived at the airport because we had been up since 4 a.m., which was 1 a.m. their time.

It didn't take long for the reality of the three-hour time difference between our areas to sink in. When our hostess picked us up, she informed us that we would be having dinner later.

Then she said, "We're having a Bible study tonight and the ladies are all looking forward to meeting you both; so if you can just try to stay up long enough to meet them, I know you would love them."

Just then I looked at my watch. It was 6:00 (our time). I was ready to eat dinner. She hadn't even begun cooking the dinner.

I said to her, "What time is it here?" and she told me that it was 3:00.

She informed me that we would be eating around 6:00. Suddenly it hit me. I thought to myself, that's 9:00 our time.

I spent the rest of the afternoon trying to keep myself busy. Finally it was time to eat and she invited us to the dining room and asked us to be seated.

As we were about to sit down at the table, she said, "Gals, would you like to hear a little opera, a little jazz, or a little country?"

I thought, "I don't care what we listen to. I just want some food." It was finally time to sit down to a good dinner as opera played softly in the background.

A moment later as I pulled my chair out to sit down there was a "weiner dog" lying there. Do you know what I mean by a "weiner dog"? I tried everything and told it everything, but it just would not move.

Finally I said to the hostess, "There's a dog laying on my feet and I can't seem to get it to move."

She said, "I can understand why. That dog belongs to my son and his family and they live in France. It only understands French."

I thought, "You've got to be kidding. 'Get out of here' doesn't have a common language?" She talked to the dog in French, it moved, and I was finally able to enjoy a lovely meal.

Following supper, she said, "Now they'll be here in a couple of hours for the Bible study."

I thought, "A couple of hours; that's getting pretty late our time. We're talking 11 p.m., and we're just getting company?"

We started the Bible study and my head began to nod, this way and that way, and I would catch myself falling asleep. It was awful. I was trying to stay interested in the Bible study but my head kept going this way and that way.

Finally, somebody said to me, "You know, Willa K., if you're getting tired you can go to bed," and I thought, "Thank you, Jesus, I am going to bed." Nancy stayed on. I don't know what time she came to bed.

The next morning we woke up at 7 a.m., which is 4 a.m. their time; everyone was sleeping. We did all that we could to entertain ourselves. We each looked through the Spiegel catalog. Nancy colored my toenails, but Nancy wouldn't let me color hers. We had to keep quiet because no one was up yet.

Finally, at 7 a.m. their time (10 a.m. our time), there was a knock on the door and our host said, "Can I get you a cup of coffee?"

I thought, "Coffee, at 10 a.m. in the morning?" Finally I said, "I'll have a Diet Coke."

When he returned with our drinks (Nancy did get coffee), he said to us that his wife was going to the hairdresser and would be back in a couple of hours. "Then we'll all go out for breakfast."

"Breakfast!" I said to Nancy. "She's going to the hairdresser and she won't be back for a couple of hours; that could be close to 1:30 our time." For the next two hours while she was gone we kept busy by looking at her California clothes catalogs. We even called some 800 numbers to order our own catalogs! When she came back I was standing by the door with my suitcase packed, but she spent a half hour doing some last minute things before we left for the retreat. Finally it was time to leave and I thought, "Now, something to eat."

Not quite yet, though. We were driving down this road and her husband said, "I think I'm lost."

"Lost," I said to myself. "This is your town and you're lost? I'm hungry." We finally got to the restaurant. It was 2:30 our time and the waitress said to us, "Lunch or breakfast?" "Oh, we'll have breakfast," said our hostess.

I don't know why I'm going on with this story; it has nothing to do with time, rather than time itself, but I know that time is important to all of us in one way or another.

When I have time to spend for enjoyment, I like going through stores where they sell bath and body oils. The only problem is that I buy a bunch of it, but when I get home, I have to use up what I already have, so I start putting on this and that and, I tell you, there are times when I go to work smelling like a fruitcake.

In a more serious thought on time, Nancy and I had a dear friend whose husband was killed at age 47. Shortly after, we resumed the Bible study at my house. We were going to do something special for her that night but she said, "No, please, not tonight. They say that part of the grieving is getting your rest, and I've been trying to do that night after night."

I thought to myself, "Isn't that what we all should do with our time?" We get tired and we try to go on for two or three hours and the next day we don't have it together. Whatever we do — shopping, going on a trip, Bible study, or prayer — we will be such better servants of God if we manage our time and keep ourselves disciplined for the task ahead.

Afterthoughts ... God talks about time in the Word. In Revelation 1:3, we read, "Blessed is he who reads and those who hear the words of this prophecy, and keep those things which are written in it; for the time is near."

The word "time" in this passage refers to an urgent call to obedience. Obedience to the Savior is all we need. Never give up! God is calling us to faithfulness and truly the time is near for His coming.

Forgiveness,
Easier Said Than Done

Who would ever think that a comment made at a ball game would initiate a five-year struggle with forgiveness?

It did for me. It happened one night when my son was involved in a T-ball game. For those of you who don't know about T-ball, it's when the ball just sits on a cylinder and the kids swing at it. When they connect they run the bases like a regular baseball game.

That particular night I was sitting on the bleachers with the other parents enjoying the game. During the game I got upset with the umpire, a young high school boy, and I said something I shouldn't have to him. I really don't know what I was upset about because in T-ball there are no balls or strikes. Another parent, a friend of mine, was sitting two rows behind me.

"Willa K., I can't believe those things are coming out of your mouth," she said.

I felt terrible. I couldn't remember what I had said. I know that I'm not a person who swears, so I know I wasn't swearing. But I must have been terribly unkind to the umpire or to somebody. I know I had been very ugly.

I went home that night and I cried and cried. I went over to see my mother and I said, "Mom, I was so bad tonight at a T-ball game. I'm going to resign all of my jobs in the church because if you can't control yourself, you can't possibly handle anything in the church."

Now my mom was a very wise person. I didn't know what she was going to say, but I knew that it was going to be good wisdom for me.

"If God wants you to resign, I think you should," she said. "But before you do anything, I want you to pray about it for two weeks."

I said, "Okay." That seemed fair enough to me.

It didn't even take the two weeks. It only took one night. The next morning (Sunday) when I got up, I thought to myself, "I had

27

every right to be upset with the umpire and my friend had no business talking to me like that."

However, each time I went to another game and saw her, I would think, "Oh, I feel so bad." But the next day I would think, "Willa K., you had every right to feel that way." It's amazing how God can tell you something one day, and then Satan can twist it around the next day.

That's how it went, back and forth, back and forth. I would love to say that this only went on for a couple of months. Unfortunately, it went on for five years. Every time I saw that lady I thought about that incident, but I wasn't going to apologize. No way. "I" was right and "she" was wrong!

I can still picture where I was standing one day in the Fair Store, a downtown variety store. I can even remember what I was doing; I was trying on gloves. Suddenly I sensed someone beside me. I looked up and there "she" was! I couldn't believe what was coming out of my mouth. "I'm so sorry for the way that I talked at the T-ball game," I said.

I thought she would say, "What T-ball game?" But that wasn't what she said. Do you know what she said?

She said, "I forgave you when it happened. I wondered, Willa K., if you would ever ask for forgiveness."

Suddenly I was aware that God had kept that on my mind all those years because He wanted me to ask for forgiveness from her. I realized that things have a wonderful ending if we allow God to have control.

That dear friend is now coming faithfully to a Bible study in my home and is one of the dearest friends that I have. Do you think I think of the T-ball game when I look at her now? Of course not, all I think of is what a wonderful friend she has become and how much we love the Lord and each other.

So I urge you, if you are holding a grudge, take care of it today. Give them a call or send them a note. The results will be unbelievable. Give yourself the gift of forgiveness. You will be surprised what a difference it makes.

Afterthought ... In Him we have redemption through His blood, the "forgiveness of sins, according to the riches of His grace." (Ephesians 1:7)

Grace, grace, God's wonderful grace. The words of this beautiful song come to mind when I think of the great love and the amazing grace that God shows to us. We are so undeserving, but he is so willing to forgive. The way of the cross leads to forgiveness. Because He walked that road to put to death our sins, because He loved so much; He provided a way out for us. Because of His great love for us!

Obedience, Coast To Coast — Border To Border

When my son, Aaron, graduated from Taylor University, he decided that during spring break he was going to join some friends traveling "coast to coast, border to border."

I'll never forget the day he told me; I had to ask what it meant.

He casually replied, "That means that in a week's time we are going to go coast to coast and border to border in a car."

I said, "You can't do that. What do the other parents have to say about this?"

"Mom, everybody is doing it," was his response.

"But you're my baby," I said. "If you must go, make sure you call me every two days. If I don't hear from you I'm calling the police and they'll track you down. I have to know where you are. When you're out there and not accountable to anybody, you guys could get run off the face of the earth and nobody would know it."

Reluctantly, he agreed to call after I said I would give him my cell phone.

So Friday of spring break rolled around and they left on this big journey! Aaron called home Saturday to let me know that they had spent the night with Tim's family in Iowa. Aaron was constantly on my mind, conscious of the fact that he was on the road. Normally I am able to sleep the night through, but Sunday night I was awakened every hour with the overwhelming feeling that I should pray for Aaron and the boys.

It was Monday at 11 a.m. when the phone rang at work. It was Aaron. It had been just two days since we had last talked.

I said, "Oh, Aaron, I'm so glad you called. Last night I was awake every hour and all I could think to do was pray for you, because you were the only person that was on my mind. Where have you been?"

"Grand Canyon," he replied.

"Was it neat?" I said.

"Yep," he responded.

31

"When did you get there?" I said.

"Last night at 9:00," he answered.

"You've been down in the canyon and back when it was dark?" I said. "How could you see in the dark?"

"Yep, the moon was shining really bright and it was neat," he replied. "The three of us just went right down there and we didn't even know where we were going, but we followed a path."

"Aaron, how foolish," I said. "What could have been in your path? At least you were with somebody."

"When I went down," was his response.

What did he mean, "When I went down"? By then I was practically in a panic over my son who was supposedly standing on the edge of the Grand Canyon two thousand miles away from me. And he was telling me that he had climbed the Grand Canyon alone in the dark.

"The guys wanted to sleep down there but I couldn't sleep on the rock so I thought I would climb back up and sleep in the car," he said.

"How long does it take to climb out?" I asked, not sure I wanted to know any more at that point.

"Four hours," he said. "But it wasn't bad. Oh, one time I saw something that was kind of big run across in front of me, but I figured if it was one of those mountain lions or something, there was nothing I could do about it anyway."

"What if you would have stepped on a snake?" I said.

"But I didn't," was his answer.

I honestly believe that I prayed that boy down the Grand Canyon and back out that night. I realized more than ever at that time the importance of being obedient to God when He asks us to pray.

Who knows why He has placed that person or prayer request on your mind. You might be sparing someone from harm or touching a life like never before. You prayed in obedience. You simply prayed because God put it on your heart.

Put it in your mind now, you'll always be blessed if you are obedient to Him. And who knows, you might be impacting for good the life of someone very close to your heart.

Afterthought ... God is calling us to obedience; obedience in our prayer life, in our ministry, to our families, and to Himself. In today's world the lack of commitment is found in so many avenues of life. We find it in commitment to spouses, children, church, jobs, and so many other parts of our life. Obedience to Christ will help us to be obedient in the other areas of our lives. When we put Christ first in all we do and ask for His guidance, He will lead us.

Today take time to talk to the Lord about your commitment to Him and then in obedience do what He asks. Always remember that God never leads us in an opposite direction than what His word tells us.

Statistics — For those of you who like statistics, here are a few from Aaron's trip. In the spring of 1997 Mike, Tim, and Aaron went 7,400 miles in 11 days, crossed 23 states, traveled into Canada and Mexico, and put their feet in the Pacific Ocean, Atlantic Ocean, and the Gulf of Mexico. They averaged 673 miles a day, drove 132 driving hours and made 26 gas stops in a little old Toyota.

Speeding:
A Red And Blue Light Special

Nancy and I and a dear friend, Maribeth, were on our way to a conference in Peoria, Illinois, which is about a six-hour drive from Berne. We have made this trip many times, so we know of certain places where we are going to stop.

Our first stop is Logansport where we use the bathroom at the J. C. Penney store. After shopping a little while we go across the road to the Wal-Mart store where we picked up some more items. By then it had gotten dark and we knew we were running late. When we left, we knew that we had to get things moving in order to arrive in Peoria on time.

I had a heavy foot but that's not unusual because I usually have a heavy foot. We came into this little town called, "Idaville," a small village where there are no speed limit signs. I remember thinking to myself, there's no speed sign here but I'll bet you have to slow down some, so I let up a little on the speed.

We continued on for three and a half miles. Suddenly, I looked in my rearview mirror and I saw red and blue lights. I immediately pulled off the road because I knew that this man was going to zoom past me because he was after somebody. Instead, he pulled off right behind me and I thought, oh no, not me!

One thing I remembered when you get pulled over, they ask whether or not you have your seat belt on. I didn't have mine on so I thought if I jump out of the van, I will not have to lie. I'll already be out and I wouldn't have to tell him I didn't have my seat belt on.

However, when I jumped out, the officer drew his gun, and I immediately put my hands up.

I said, "What did I do? What did I do?"

He said, "Lady, just get back in the van."

I said, excitedly by then, "I'll get in the van. I'll get in the van."

I got in the van and he said, "I'd like to see your driver's license."

I replied, "I know you'd like to see my driver's license. I'll get it out of my purse. I know where it is. I always have it in my purse in the same place all of the time. If I can just get out my billfold, I know that I'll be able to find it."

Unfortunately, it wasn't where I thought it should be, so I continued to search frantically. All along, he stood there and looked on with a rather stoic expression. However, I kept talking, faster and faster!

"Now where could it be," I said as I totally came unglued. "Oh, I know where it is. We just came back from California and I had to show my 'ID' all the time at the airports. If you'll just wait a little bit I'll get it out, and then I can show it to you and you'll be able to see it."

Finally I found it. I opened up my purse and took it out and said, "Here it is."

He said, "Thank you."

Then he said, "Now I would like to see your registration."

With the same sense of frustration I replied, "Oh, I know that it's right here. My husband would never send me on the road without a registration. I know exactly where it is. It's always right above the visor."

Unfortunately, this time it wasn't. I searched everywhere, but I couldn't come up with the registration.

"I'm sorry," I said. "I didn't know that I wouldn't be able to find it. It must be in the glove box. Nancy, check the glove box. Is it in there?"

It wasn't in there, or the next several places where we looked.

"My husband is not that kind of a man," I said in desperation. "I know it's somewhere in here. Just give me a chance to look for it. Really, I know it's here. If you'll just give me a chance, I've got a cell phone and I can call my husband to see if he knows where it is. He'll tell me right where things are and I can show it to you. My husband would never send me on the road without the registration!"

All of a sudden the officer said, with firmness in his voice, "Lady, be quiet! Just go. Just go and watch your speed."

I said, "Oh, I will. Thank you so much, officer."

As we pulled away, Nancy said to Maribeth, "Did you see that police officer following us?"

I couldn't believe it — like Maribeth would have seen the police officer coming and wouldn't say anything. Oh, we had a brilliant conversation in the van.

For the next five miles that police officer followed me. Do you know how hard it is to go 55 miles per hour when there are curves here and there and you don't know the road? Finally, he turned off the road to go to McDonald's.

Isn't that a lot like our prayer life sometimes? We get so busy praying to God about everything we want to say that we don't listen, or even notice that He is around. We never once stop to listen to see what He has for us or what He would like to tell us.

Don't you think at times He must feel like that officer? Do you think He would like to say, "Just be quiet, I would like to talk to you?" I realized more than ever after that episode on the way to Peoria how patient God is; how He allows us to go our own way and how much grace He has for each one of us.

As we drove toward Peoria, I found myself silently saying, "Lord, make me less of a talker and more of a listener. Help me to hear what you have to say to me right now."

Afterthought ... A favorite verse that always gives me peace comes from the book of Psalms 46. "God is our refuge and strength, a very present help in trouble. Therefore we will not fear ... be still, and know that I am God; I will be exalted among the nations. I will be exalted in the earth!"

Just like the psalmist, David, we can know this kind of peace in our lives. Sometimes it is very hard to be quiet, especially in a world traveling so fast around us. So many places to go, people to see, and things to do it is hard to stop what we are doing and just be quiet in the presence of God. This verse is telling us that God will be exalted even in a battle we have no chance of winning. God is with us; He is reliable; He is our stronghold, and nothing in the future can give us cause to fear.

Wherefore Art Thou, O Wig!

Every morning I pray, "Lord, help me to be an example to someone today and be a shining light in this dark world. I want this day to make a difference for your Kingdom."

This particular morning I had gotten up for the third morning in a row and I was having the same problem. My doctor had told me that if I have the same problem for the third day in a row I would have to go to the hospital. I was willing to go but when I looked in the mirror I knew I had to do something with my hair. At that time wigs were really fashionable so I decided to put mine on. I left for the doctor's office anticipating the worst.

When I arrived at the doctor's office, he suggested doing the "procedure" at his office. Had I known what he was going to do I would have elected to go to the operating room! As most women know, procedures and male doctors don't always go together. When the doctor says to a woman, "This won't hurt." How does he know? He doesn't have a clue!

I still can hear the words of the doctor, "This (pain) will begin to get worse and worse. At the point it really gets bad...." He hesitated, and then he finally said, "Do you sing?"

I said, "Yes."

"Then I suggest you start singing when it really gets bad," the doctor said.

It was really more than I could take. But as the procedure went along, it started to hurt more and more.

He said, "It's hurting, isn't it?"

I said, "Yes."

He replied, "Go ahead and sing."

Without thinking, this is what I sang to my gynecologist,

> *"If it takes forever, I will wait for you.*
> *For a thousand hours, I will wait for you."*

All of a sudden, it dawned on me! What was I singing? I quickly switched to,

*"Rescue the perishing; care for the dying.
Jesus is merciful, Jesus will save."*

It was already too late to save me! I was to the point where it didn't hurt anymore! I just felt awful! I kept wondering what the doctor thought of me. What was he going to tell his wife when he got home? I could just hear him saying, "You won't believe what this woman in the office did today. She was singing love songs to me as I did a 'procedure' on her."

I didn't say anymore, and I closed my eyes so I wouldn't have to see him. The procedure finally ended and the doctor helped me sit up. I thought, "Finally, it's over." But *something* wasn't right.

Suddenly I knew what was wrong. I didn't have my wig on! It was still lying on the table. So I leaned back on the table and thrust my head back into my wig. When I sat back up the bangs were about down in my eyes.

"Does he know?" I thought. "Well, he has to know because he helped me sit up. Does he know how awful my hair looks? I'll never be able to face him again."

He sat down at his desk with his back to me and I sat on the edge of the table. He wrote some things down, but he never turned my direction. I didn't say a word, either. Finally, he got up and never looked back. He just left the room.

"Thank you, Jesus," I said quietly to myself.

I didn't know what to do, so out of embarrassment I started to laugh. I laughed and I laughed, mainly from nervousness. I can't tell you how awful I felt.

Suddenly the door opened and in came the doctor.

"What's so funny?" he asked.

I did not know what to say but I knew that I wasn't going to give him the satisfaction of knowing that I knew that he knew that I knew.

I replied, "Isn't it amazing how good we feel when it's all over?" That's all I said and that was all that I was going to say. I never did

40

see that man again and I wasn't going to go back to that doctor. Eventually he moved. I always wondered whether or not he wanted to move on somewhere where they have real people, more normal people.

It was all so humbling to me. That very morning I had prayed, "Lord, help me to be an example and a witness for you." What did that doctor think? Did he think that I would wait a thousand hours for him?

I was totally humiliated and so disappointed. Once again I had failed God and I had to confess my downfalls to the Lord. It is so hard to do that. We don't like to admit that we fail or that we are wrong. But as humiliating as it is, it is absolutely essential to empty ourselves if we are going to have an effective prayer life.

Afterthought ... There are times we disappoint the Lord in our actions. A few Sunday's ago our lesson in Sunday school centered around the verse, "even a child is known by his doings." This is true even with adults. As children of the King we are known by our doings, also. Even in those times when we disappoint Him, or think we have disappointed Him, He still loves us.

We must remain steadfast and hold on to the beliefs that have been instilled in our hearts. Times will come when we make mistakes, but we must not give up. We would never let our children quit just because they made a mistake. The Lord feels the same way about us. He wants us to try over and over again. He will give us the courage to remain bold in our witness as we continue to seek Him for our strength.

Would You Be Interested In Marrying Me?

When I think of thanksgiving, I think of my husband. He was the best looking man around. All of the girls wanted to go out with him; he didn't seem interested in any of them. Even my neighbor wanted to go with him.

One Sunday my neighbor, Pat, and I spent the day together. After church on Sunday evening we were riding around when we ran into Lee. We stopped to visit and we invited him over to Pat's house to watch TV with us. (In Berne, there is not much more you can do on a Sunday night.) I knew how bad she wanted to go with him, so I thought I would help them get together. I thought that he was a good-looking guy.

When we got to her home we went into the TV room where I sat down on one sofa and Pat sat on the other. Lee then sat down on the sofa I was sitting on. I was surprised but I didn't know what to do, so we just watched TV. Pat's parents returned so I went to say goodbye. I was shocked when Lee said, "I will take you home."

My first thought was, "Oh, I've really offended my neighbor now," so I said, "I just live next door and there's no need to drive me home."

He said, "I know where you live."

To that I replied, "I can walk next door."

But he said, "Oh, it has snowed, let me take you home."

We went back and forth with me saying, "No," and him saying, "Yes."

Well, he took me home and then we didn't see each other for a few days. I remember looking out our window and seeing his car at Pat's house one evening and feeling a little disappointed, but I didn't know why. Then, a couple of weeks later, I met him on the street just a block from where we are living today. He was driving one way and I was driving the other.

He flagged me down. When I rolled down my window he said, "Would you be interested in marrying me?"

I said, "You've got to be kidding!"

He acknowledged that he was, but then he said, "If I can find somebody to marry me in the next two weeks, I don't have to go to the army. Otherwise, I will be leaving in a couple of weeks." We made small talk after that but I can't remember what was really said, as I was still thinking about his initial question.

Two nights before he was going to leave for the army, I was standing out in the yard and he pulled up. He wanted to know if I would go out with him the next night, and I said, "Yes."

Then something happened for the first time in all of my years of dating. He got out of the car and kissed me! What a surprise!

"My parents are having a party and so I won't be able to come before 8 p.m." Lee said.

I said that was okay with me and he walked me to the back door.

He kissed me again. We hadn't even gone out. Then he told me that he would see me tomorrow night at 7:30!

I thought, "Wow, I must really have a powerful kiss. We've gone from 8:00 to 7:30."

Next he walked me to the breezeway door. And then he kissed me again. Then he said, "I'll see you tomorrow night at 7:00."

Boy, was I good or was I good!

The next evening 7:00 rolled around and he didn't come, and I began crying.

My mom said, "I know, Willa K., I've heard this story over and over. You wish you wouldn't be going on a date because now you are going to have to go out and look like you are having a good time. If you were with your friends, you would know that you were having fun."

I said, "No, Mom, I really want to go out with Lee." Three minutes later he came and we had a wonderful time together.

The next morning he left for Fort Knox, Kentucky. A few days later he called. Ironically, the day he called me, I was standing uptown watching Amos and Nancy's apartment burn, but I didn't know Nancy at the time.

When I got home my mom said, "There was a phone call for you and he said he was going to call back later. We think it's the boy you went out with."

I couldn't believe it. Why would he call me all the way from Fort Knox? I received the answer later that evening when he called back and asked me to come and see him.

My mother was a good seamstress. She sewed this beautiful lemon colored linen dress, with a coat to match. We went to the shoe store and got new shoes and to the jewelry store to purchase some jewelry to match. I was going to look as nice as I could for him when we met. I felt like a million dollars when I went to see this guy I had only dated once.

I stayed at his parent's home so we could leave early Sunday morning and all three of us got into the front seat of the car. Cars were bigger then and I was smaller, too. We were off for Fort Knox. His parents were Nazarene. When we got about ten miles out of Berne, his mother started to talk about the Nazarene beliefs.

She said, "We don't believe in makeup or jewelry."

I knew right away that I was in trouble. Finally, we stopped at a restroom near Pendleton, Indiana. His mother went in first and I went next. I went in a Mennonite and came out a Nazarene. I had taken off my new jewelry and washed off a lot of my makeup. I wanted to look the way his mother thought I should look.

When we got to Fort Knox, we noted right away the army had shaved off all the hair on their heads. All of these men were walking our way and my future mother-in-law said, "Oh, there he is, there he is. He's coming toward us."

I didn't dispute that but I wasn't quite sure which one he was. I had only been out on one date with him and he didn't look the same. These men all looked alike. Same haircuts, same clothes, which one was Lee? I wasn't sure which one he was. Everyone looked the same but I knew that he was one of them. Suddenly three soldiers broke away and came directly toward us. "The one with a big smile," I thought, "this must be him!"

There was no doubt, and then his mother said, "Go ahead and kiss her. I know that's what you want to do anyway."

Well, Lee and I married three months after he returned home. You never forget the first time that you met your husband, and how wonderful that time was. Do you remember how thankful you were?

45

That's the thanksgiving we should have in our hearts every day for our Heavenly Father. He is so special. I can only liken it to how special my husband is to me. Love that is so unconditional and embracing, that just makes us want to say, "Thank you, God."

Afterthought ... The word love always brings to my mind I Corinthians 13, often referred to as "the love chapter" in the Bible. In my Bible I have underlined the words of verse 7, "bears all things, believes all things, hopes all things, endures all things." In red I have written the words, "If you love someone you will always expect the best from him or her."

We often ask the question, "How will I know who the right person is for me?" I remember some old words said a long time ago. They were, "Keep your mouth shut and your ears open." Then we can wait upon the Lord to speak to us. Don't go and ask everyone you know what should I do, what should I do? Just wait upon the Lord to show you the way, and He will!

Lee and Willa K. didn't date a long time before they knew they loved each other and became engaged. God has a way of sparking the fire in our hearts for the one He has for our life partner. He (Jesus) knows the words from I Corinthians by heart. He lived them upon the cross!

Goldilocks And The Three Bears
Part 1 — No Place To Stay

Nancy and I have the opportunity to travel all over. We have gone coast to coast and border to border, and we just love it when we can go and share the love of Jesus. Every so often when we stay at a distance they ask us if we would like to stay in a motel. To be honest, if we have any say-so in it, that is our preference. Sometimes when we go, we stay in people's homes.

This particular time we had driven a couple of hours but we were going to be in the area the next night so we were asked if they could share expenses for the Mothers Day banquet at their churches. We arrived in the small town eagerly waiting to speak that evening. As customary we stopped at a convenience store so we could get ourselves together. We quickly straightened our dresses and put on a little more make-up, hoping we would look refreshed when we arrived.

As we arrived, we knew by the church sign that this was the place we were supposed to be at. As we pulled into the parking lot, we immediately noticed that it was a very beautiful church.

Nancy and I walked into this beautiful facility and we stood and stood and stood. We stood for fifteen minutes and no one spoke to us. I thought of the lady who had contacted me. It was all by mail and by phone, so she didn't know me and I didn't know her. I thought she might be getting nervous as to whether or not her speaker was there. Surely she would be coming over and saying something to us sooner or later, but nobody came. People were beginning to sit down at the tables to eat. I said to Nancy, "Let's not miss out on the food. We'd better sit down."

We found an empty table just two rows from the front. Other ladies soon came to our table but no one sat around us. I asked Nancy, "Did you put on deodorant today?"

"Of course I did," she said in disgust.

In just a short time someone got up and asked the blessing. Soon after that the tables were dismissed by rows and it was finally our turn to go through the buffet line. Something happened to us that hadn't happened all evening; someone spoke to us! It was one of the caterers asking, "Do you want au gratin or scalloped potatoes?" By that time we were so excited that someone spoke to us that we took a little of both.

We continued to sit there at the table all by ourselves until it was time for the program to begin. A young lady got up and gave a little recitation and another girl presented special music. Finally, someone got up and said, "We're so pleased to have Willa K. Sprunger from Berne, Indiana." I leaned over to Nancy and said, "Well, this is the right place."

I told my stories and sat back down at the table. At the close of the banquet, the pastor's wife came up and told us that they had made arrangements for us to stay, and that our hostess would be coming in a few minutes to take us to her home.

Finally, a lady came up to me and said, "You'll be going home with me tonight. I'm on the cleanup committee and so you're going to have to wait until I'm finished!"

I said, "Sure, we'll be glad to wait." I mean, what was I going to say, "No, I'm not going to wait. You'll have to take me right now." I could tell she was not a happy camper.

The pastor's wife came and asked us to join her and her husband as they gave us a tour of the facilities. When we returned, our hostess came over to us and said, "Well, I'm ready. You'll have to stay close to me because I live in a subdivision and if you don't stay close you'll lose me."

I thought, "Whoa." I got in the van and I said to Nancy, "Boy, are we in for a treat tonight, but what can we do now? We can't change anything. We're going to this lady's house."

We drove through the subdivision, turning this way and that way. Nancy said, "I wonder if we'll ever find our way out of here tomorrow morning?"

To that I replied, "Hey, that's no problem. We'll definitely find our way out. We've got bigger problems tonight!"

When we arrived at her house, we immediately understood why she didn't seem to be happy about having us spend the night. There were lots of cars in front of her home.

When we entered her home she introduced us to her husband, her two children, her married daughter and husband, her three grandchildren, and her mother and father! My immediate thought was, "Where am I going to sleep tonight with all of these people in the house? Why didn't they just send us to a motel for the night?"

Her parents escorted us into the kitchen. Just then the back door opened and there stood the pastor's wife. She brought potato chips and some soda. We had a nice visit with her parents and the pastor's wife. When it was time for us to go to bed, the hostess came into the kitchen and said, "You will be sleeping in the first bedroom on the left at the top of the stairs."

Nancy went up ahead of me and I joined her a few minutes later. When I went into the room, Nancy said, "We've got a real problem."

I said, "I know. She doesn't want us here."

Nancy replied, "No, no, we've got a different problem. We've got an old bed."

I said, "So what's so bad about an old bed? We've slept in old beds before."

She said, "There are slats underneath here and I don't think the bed is going to hold us."

I checked underneath the bed and sure enough, I could see what she was talking about. We decided to adjust the slats. I got down under the bed and put the slats evenly on the rails so it would hold us. Then we thought, "What if we have to get up in the night?" I said to Nancy, "Once we get in this bed, we're not going to be able to move. You can't roll over; the way you get into bed is the way you are going to stay all night. We cannot move or the bed may collapse."

Then we discovered a new problem. I might have to get up in the night. I said, "Let's move the bed out a little from the wall so I can get out if I must. I don't dare roll over you. If I do, that puts all of the weight on one side of the bed and for sure it will go down. If you think she's unhappy now, wait until that happens!"

Just when we thought we had things taken care of, we moved the bed so we could get around it and discovered that there were little tacks all around the outside of the room. They were getting ready to lay new carpet. I told Nancy, "Get out all the shoes you brought and we will line them up around the room so I won't step on the tacks if I need to get out of bed in the night." And so we lined up our shoes around the room.

Just then, there was a knock on the door. It was our hostess.

"Ladies, I forgot to tell you one thing. Because of all the people in the house, we are asking that you use the bathroom between 8:00 and 8:30 in the morning."

"Oh, um, um, thank you," I said, but inside we were nervous wrecks. My bladder can't tell time. I mean, what was I going to do?

We went to bed and in the end we slept pretty well. For the first time in our lives, neither one of us had to get up in the night. In the morning we sat there until it was "our time." But I tell you, at exactly 8 a.m., did we ever take off for the bathroom!

We packed our bags and headed downstairs where we discovered that the pastor's wife had brought donuts, orange juice, and a thermos of coffee to us. However, we noticed something else as we looked to another part of the house. There was our hostess and around her were little children. She had been up since 6 a.m. running a day care center in her home. Needless to say, we ate our breakfast and exited the home!

As we look back on that situation now, we realize that she truly was a wonderful hostess. She had allowed us to come into her home even when she had so many people there. She had made quite a sacrifice for us all.

At the time, however, we had felt totally unwanted and rejected. That's kind of the way Goldilocks was when she went into the first bed. It didn't feel comfortable to her.

Goldilocks And The Three Bears
Part 11 — The Billets

The second bed Goldilocks tried out was one that was a little too soft. It just wasn't comfortable for her. That describes the second place where we stayed, which was in Canada.

Going into Canada takes a little bit of an adjustment, even though they speak English like we do. It's the way they say certain things. They say, "aboat," rather than "about." For them, a napkin is a serviette.

After our program at the church, they handed me a list of who would be staying together at each home. Our hostess was a lovely lady named Mavis who was wearing a beautiful white coat. She stood in the foyer of the church waiting for us. I thought, how fortunate we are to be going home with her.

As she approached us I said, "You must be Mrs. Billets. My name is Willa K. Sprunger."

She said, "No, you are the Billets."

I thought she hadn't heard me correctly so I said again, "My name is Willa K. Sprunger and you must be Mrs. Billets?"

She said again, "No, you are the Billets."

This time I was sure she must have a hearing problem so I said loudly, "MY NAME IS WILLA K. SPRUNGER."

She laughed and said, "In Canada when you are a guest you are a billet."

Big deal! Why doesn't someone just tell us we are a billet?

She wanted to know if we would have any trouble following her and we told her that we are seasoned drivers in subdivisions. Still, it seemed like we drove and drove. We turned and we turned but she always waited at the red lights for us, guiding us until we finally drove in front of this house, a big house! I had never in my life seen such a big home.

Nancy and I went into the house and walked into the foyer. I can't begin to describe how big it was. The foyer was bigger than my living room and my living room is the half the original house!

Then we went into one of the living rooms that went into another living room that went into the kitchen. The kitchen was so big that it had an island in the middle so huge that Nancy and I could have pitched a tent on it and camped there for the night.

Our hostess asked us, "Would you girls like to have a little something to eat before you go to bed?"

As proper Canadians would say, I said, "I would love to."

She said, "We'll go into the parlor where we can have a little bite to eat before we retire for the night."

We went into the parlor and sat down. She brought me this little cup of tea. It was the smallest cup I had ever seen. It was really, really small, just two slurps and you were done. She also brought us a little petit four, one bite and it was gone. Boy, I was used to something with a little more substance, like a Ho Ho or a Twinkie and a Diet Coke! I tried so hard to cross my legs like Mavis did; she was a wonderful hostess. But I just couldn't! I was so much bigger!

We had a beautiful visit and learned many wonderful things about the life of this lovely lady, Mavis.

Finally she said, "Let me take you to your rooms."

We followed her up the stairs and at the top she said, "This is our bedroom where my husband and I sleep." I thought, "Who cares!" No one has ever said that to us before! Then she said to me, "You can have the room next to us. Now let me show you Nancy's room."

We walked down a long catwalk where we could look down into the two living rooms on either side of the walk. When we arrived at a bedroom on the other side of the home she said, "Now, Nancy, this is your bedroom."

Only one thing about this arrangement bothered me. Now I am going to share something with you that I would appreciate you would not pass along. I snore. I snore really loud! I didn't want to sleep next to the hostess and her husband because I didn't want to disturb them or keep them from sleeping because of my snoring.

Finally I said, "You know, I'm just not comfortable sleeping in a room by myself. Do you mind if Nancy and I share a bedroom? We are used to staying together."

She responded, "No, if you're comfortable, that's fine."

Nancy and I opened up the door of the bedroom and we couldn't believe what we saw. I mean it was a picture out of *Better Homes and Gardens*, a dream house you wouldn't mind having someday. The cover of the bed matched the curtains, the curtains matched the sofa, and sofa matched the design in the carpet. We thanked her for the lovely room.

After we closed the door, Nancy said, "Can you imagine staying in this place?"

I said, "No, this is unbelievable. Can you imagine her cleaning this? And she doesn't have Amish girls! I'll bet she doesn't clean it. I bet she's got a cleaning lady."

Just then there was a knock on the door. It was our hostess.

I thought, "Oh no, here it comes; we're going to have to pay for our room."

She said, "If for any reason you have to get up during the night, you will need to wake my husband or me. I will be setting an alarm system. If anyone steps on the stairway, the alarm will go off immediately and the police will be here in a matter of moments."

We must have looked dumfounded because she said, "Oh, I must have forgotten to tell you...." I thought, "Here it comes ... something bad!" "My husband is vice president of the Dow Chemical Corporation and they are on strike right now. We've had several threats at our house."

Nancy and I closed the door.

I told Nancy, "Oh, I think I had better call Lee. I want him to know what we were doing the last night that we were here." By that time I was really wondering what we had gotten into. Are they going to blow us up? Are we even going to see the light of day?

We didn't talk much after that. We just kind of went to bed when all of a sudden we heard a scary noise. It was terrifying!

And I whispered, "Nancy, did you hear that?"

She said softly, "Yes."

I said in a quiet voice, "What is it?"

She whispered, "I don't know but I hear it too."

"Oh, I was hoping you hadn't heard the noise," I said quietly.

Softly she said, "I do, I do, but I don't know what it is."

By that time we both admitted that we were scared. All of a sudden, I heard that noise again, and I said in a small voice, "Someone's coming! What are we going to do?"

I kid you not; this is what Nancy said, "Let's get under the bed."

"Under the bed? Look at us. We are big people! How are we going to get under the bed?"

Then Nancy said, "Let's lay still and pull the covers over our heads."

We continued to hear the noise, but eventually we fell fast asleep.

In the morning we woke up in our beautiful room and we were still alive! We opened the curtains and looked out the window and discovered a most beautiful view. There we were, right on the shore of Lake Huron. Now I know what you're thinking: it was the waves making that noise. Maybe it was and maybe it wasn't! Maybe someone had come but they took one look and LEFT!

We went downstairs and shared a lovely breakfast with Mavis in her breakfast nook. I had never eaten in a breakfast nook before, and I want you to know that food tastes the same in a breakfast nook as it does at the table. We shared from God's Word and prayed before leaving and said our goodbyes.

Nancy and I pulled away. I looked at her and she looked at me.

Finally I said, "What do you think?"

Nancy said, "She was very nice, but I wasn't comfortable. It certainly wasn't what I'm used to."

Just like Goldilocks who was trying to find the "perfect fit" for her bed, we hadn't been comfortable with our surroundings either.

Goldilocks And The Three Bears
Part III — Just Like Home

Our third place to land in Goldilocks fashion was at the home of a dear friend in Peoria. Linda Maricle, a close friend in women's ministries, had invited us to stay overnight with her during a meeting in that area.

After traveling for hours, we pulled up to Linda's doorstep that afternoon. There was a surprise waiting for us. When she had invited us to stay, she hadn't told us that her home was under a major renovation project. I thought that was a perfect time to have your guests stay at a motel.

The first thing we noticed is that there were no front door steps. Just when we were wondering how we were going to get in, Linda opened the door. She said, "Come on in."

I said, "We'd love to but there are no steps." She welcomed us, reaching out her hand and literally pulling us inside her home.

Upon entering the house, the first thing we noticed was this huge room with absolutely nothing in it. It was just being completed as an addition to the house. As a result, everything was covered with drywall dust. Everywhere we looked there was a deposit of the dust an inch thick.

The kitchen was packed with things because of the project. The kitchen table was loaded with everything, as were the counters and everything in between. All we could see was the kitchen sink and the top of the stove.

Finally, she invited us into the living room and the situation there was even worse. Even the sofa had things piled all over it. Things were piled so high I couldn't see across the room from me because of the dining room table piled high in the middle of the room.

As I looked at this construction mess around me, I began to wonder whether or not Linda had the right day for our arrival. Why would she want guests to come when it was such a mess? But none of that meant anything to her.

She said, "Girls, have a seat wherever you can find one. My folks heard you were coming and they want to visit with you, too. So I invited them over for dinner."

Another thought I had was, "Where are we going to have dinner?" There was no place on the dining room table to eat. However, in her own way, Linda knew what she was doing. She started taking things off of the table. She even decorated it with her best linens and fine china. I couldn't believe it. This was truly a "Chinette" moment if there ever was one.

Just then the doorbell rang and she said to her husband, "Steve, would you get the door?"

His reply was, "I'd rather not. It's just my mother-in-law."

He went to the door and pulled them into the house in the same way Linda had done with us. We sat down ready for a wonderful meal. Just when we were bowing our heads to give thanks, I heard the word, "Yuck." I looked up and it was her son. He didn't like casseroles, and that's what we were having for supper. Moments later as Linda's hand went under the table I heard, "Ouch!"

Linda said to Steve, "Can you do something about your son?"

Steve replied, "I think it's a little late. The ladies already know how he feels about your meal."

I thought to myself, "This is just like home!"

Following dinner, Linda took us to the place where we ministered that evening. When the service was over, Nancy and I went on ahead to the car and I said, "Where do you think we are going to sleep tonight?"

Nancy replied, "I don't know why you worry about things like that."

I said, "Did you look in their rooms?"

"No," she said.

"Well, I did," I told her. "If you go into her daughter's room, there's not enough room to get to the bed. If you go in the son's room, there is only a path to the bed."

Nancy told me not to worry about such things, but I told her that I wanted to know where I was sleeping that night.

Shortly after, Linda got into the car and we had to stop our conversation. After all, you can't talk about people when they are right there. My mom told me, you just don't do that!

The first thing she said when she got in the car was, "Would you girls like to go home and have some pizza?"

I thought, "Well, she's just trying to put off going to bed because there's no place for us to sleep. We're just going to sit up all night."

Finally, she offered to show us to our room for the night. As we went down the hall to the bedroom we couldn't believe she was giving her bedroom to us. It had a king-sized waterbed, but that is not what caught my eye as we walked into the bedroom. It was the headboard. I looked at Linda and said, "Let me ask you a question. Is that a cemetery gate?"

Her answer was, "Oh, yes, that has real sentimental value to our family. The cemetery where that came from is where my husband's grandparents are buried."

I thought, "Who cares? Do you mean I'm going to be putting my head down at the cemetery gate tonight?" That didn't sound like a good thought to me.

I said, "Where are you and Steve going to sleep?"

She replied, "Don't you worry about that. We'll be fine." To this day, I don't have any idea where they slept or even had room to lay down for the night.

As we got into bed, we noticed that there was a new bathroom off of our room. Since it wasn't quite finished, Linda had decorated the doorway with a curtain so that the room would look nicer for us to sleep there.

I said to Nancy, "Look, we've got a brand new bathroom."

Just then there was a knock on the door and it was Linda. She said, "Don't use the new bathroom. Everything is there but it's not hooked up yet." I thought, "I'm glad she told me now before I used the new toilet!"

We went to bed and Nancy said, "Do you mind if I read?"

I said, "No, that's fine. I'm tired because I'm the one that drove to Peoria, so I think I'm going to go to sleep." Immediately I fell into a deep sleep.

All of a sudden something went running across my face and I sat up and screamed, "What was that? What was that? What was that, Nancy? What was that thing that just ran across my face?"

Nancy tried to "shush" me but it didn't work. I screamed even louder and she tried to quiet me down again.

"It's only a cat," she said. "It's nothing to get upset about."

"What do you mean it is nothing to get upset about?" I screamed. "I wasn't raised in a house where there were cats. I'm not used to a cat climbing all over the bed like this."

I went to the door and called, "Linda, there's a kitty in here."

She said, "Oh, you naughty Whitney, come here."

My words echoed hers as I replied, "Yes, you naughty Whitney."

She told us to send the cat out.

"I can't believe you're making such a big fuss over a cat," said Nancy.

"What would you have done if it had run over your face?" I said. "You're just sitting over there reading. It's a lot different for you."

I couldn't understand why Nancy was so casual about it. I care about *her*. When they showed us the room and I saw that we were sleeping in a waterbed, I cared immediately because Nancy can't swim and I never brought the swimmies! What was I going to do if she drowned in the night? How was I going to tell Amos that we lost her in a waterbed?

We tried it again, but it didn't work. Back in came the cat. This time it just laid its white furry head beside mine on the pillow, like she was settling in for the night. It wasn't that I didn't like her. She was a pretty cat, a white angora cat. It's just that I didn't want her sleeping with me in the same bed.

I got up and called Linda again and her response was the same, "Just send her out."

It was obvious that wasn't working, so I said to Nancy, "I know where she is coming from. She's going into that other bathroom and climbing through the new bathroom. We're going to have to close off that bathroom. Did you bring the muumuu that your mother made you twenty years ago?"

Nancy is the kind of person that puts on a robe if she gets up in the night. She likes to be fully covered to go to the bathroom. I'm the type of person that if I have to go, I'm on my way.

"Let's pin that muumuu to the bottom of the curtain," I said to Nancy. "Then we can move a dresser up against it to make sure that cat doesn't get in."

"I am having no part of moving furniture," said Nancy.

I said, "We are putting the dresser next to it."

Again she said, "I will have no part in moving furniture."

This time Willa K. firmly said, "WE ARE MOVING THE DRESSER!"

Finally, she gave in and we pushed the dresser against the curtain and we slept the night through.

When we got up in the morning, we went out to a wonderful breakfast where Linda had once again set the table as if we were queens. We were visiting and Linda said, "I'll bet that the cat didn't bother you any more, did she?"

I thought, "Oh, no, she knows that we moved the furniture and she's going to be upset." We had tried to be so quiet hoping she would not hear.

Nancy said, "No, we slept just fine."

"I knew she wouldn't because I put her in the basement," Linda said.

"Oh, no, all that work for nothing," I thought.

Linda told us of the beauty along the river in Peoria at that time of year, and she insisted that we take a drive before we left for Indiana. So we did and saw the beauty of God's handiwork that morning.

As we drove away we felt cared for and loved. There she was, in the midst of a renovation project, and yet she opened her home warmly to friends. Her actions had proven her beautiful friendship in spite of the circumstances that could have made it otherwise. In spite of all this, we had felt at home there. We left there realizing that it wasn't things, or experiences, but her friendship that had made all the difference.

Goldilocks And The Three Bears
Part IV — Just Right

Why did I tell these three stories and what did they have to do with "Goldilocks And The Three Bears"? Their progression is very similar to that old childhood story from our past. The first two beds weren't right for Goldilocks, but she fell asleep in the third bed and was "still there" when the bears came home.

In the first story, we felt like we had been totally rejected. That is how the Heavenly Father feels when He wants to come into our heart and we say, "Not now, not now." We say that the time isn't right; we're too busy, or we want to wait until we're older. Have you rejected Christ's invitation to come into your heart?

There was absolutely nothing wrong with the second place. It was a beautiful home; it's just that we didn't feel comfortable in it.

There are times when you really aren't comfortable with your Christian experience. There are other things coming between you and God and you really aren't committed to Him at the time. I've found out in the past few months that my walk with Christ can be so much more when I spend time in prayer and in His Word. The older I get, the more I care about the things that are important.

I have discovered the importance of having devotions and prayer in the morning. That was something I didn't do on a regular basis. Do you know why? My life was so busy doing the work of the Lord that I thought that could replace a daily prayer and Bible study. Oh, I would have prayer or Bible reading, but I was not faithful. God constantly prompted me to spend more time with Him and I would, for a couple of days, but then my busy schedule let me forget about my commitment to Him. I would tell people that I would pray for them, then I would forget about the request. Recently, my life has completely changed because I've discovered the power that comes in being a praying woman.

The last place we visited was just like home. It was just as relaxed as the last bed where Goldilocks plopped down and fell fast asleep. When we know Jesus as our Savior, God blesses us with real peace.

One new dimension in my prayer life has been the use of my computer. I e-mail my children every Monday morning and ask them what I can pray for in their lives that week. The prayer requests I received from them have been amazing.

I've found that such prayer is a two-way street. Not only is it a blessing in my life because I'm praying for the request, but it's a blessing for my children as they see how God cares about every aspect of their lives, including the littlest concerns. They are discovering that God cares about everything because they are seeing Him work in all things.

In a sense, there are three things that Goldilocks learned that we could apply to our spiritual lives. First, if we have never accepted Christ as our Savior, we are lost in sin and need to take care of that part of our lives. "For the wages of sin is death, but the gift of God is eternal life through Jesus Christ our Lord." [Romans 6:23] To receive forgiveness all you need to do is pray this simple prayer of salvation:

> *"Lord, I know I'm a sinner and I need to be forgiven of my sins. I ask you now to cleanse me from every sin. Come into my heart and live in me. Help me to be obedient to your Word and put you first in my life.*
> *In Jesus' Name. Amen"*

Secondly, if we are struggling with our commitment to Jesus Christ, we need to change our ways and seek the power of prayer. Thirdly, if we are at peace spiritually, then we need to keep on praying, studying God's Word, and minister with the gifts God has given each one of us.

Service With A Smile

When we think of Christian service, what are we thinking about? Is it teaching Sunday school or serving in some special position in the church? Is that what we think of when we think of serving God?

For me, it was brought home very plainly one day when I went to the grocery store. There was a wonderful checkout lady by the name of Dixie. I loved her. She was just the nicest person, and I loved to get in her lane when I went to the store.

That particular morning I was standing in Dixie's line. I was the third person in line, trying to add up in my head how much I had spent, making sure I had a coupon for the items I was buying. When it was my turn to check out my groceries, I looked at her and I said, "How are you today?"

To my surprise, great big tears welled up in her eyes and she started to cry. I said, "Oh, Dixie, what's wrong?"

She replied, "Things are going badly at my house right now. I wasn't going to come to work today, but then I thought to myself, 'Maybe Willa K. will come through my line today.'"

I thought to myself, "Me come through the line today?" I go to the grocery store about once a week, and I'm in the line for two or three minutes, and she thought "me come through her line? She was looking forward to me coming through her line?"

The gift of service has nothing to do with teaching Sunday school or holding any special position in the church. It has to do with the fact that you can be an encouragement wherever you are. The scary part is that you don't even know where that is most of the time.

The meeting with Dixie that morning was a real reminder to me that, no matter what I am doing, God is using me. I had no clue. Shortly after that, Dixie moved away and I have lost contact with her. When I think of her, I pray for her. Her comment when I went through the line that day makes me aware of my responsibility in everything I do.

It's not always easy to be on your best behavior, especially in checkout lines. Don't you get impatient when the person in front of you can't tell the difference between a quarter and a nickel? Don't you want to hurry them along?

Now I'm the one who can't tell the difference between a quarter and a nickel. I'm the one who has to get them out and weigh them in my hand. I'm sure there are some young girls waiting behind me who say, "Can't she tell the difference?"

We need to be aware that we are in the service of the King no matter where we are, the grocery store, the department store, everywhere. We never know who the next "Dixie" is who will look to us for a connection to God's encouragement for that day. We will never know when we will be called into service; sometimes in the most unexpected situations.

Afterthought ... One of the most popular books today in secular and religious bookstores is *The Prayer of Jabez*, authored by Bruce Wilkinson. The simple prayer of a man who is only spoken of one time in the Bible is transforming lives around the world. The words of the prayer in I Chronicles 4:9 and 10 say, "Oh, that You would bless me indeed, and enlarge my territory, that Your hand would be with me, and that You would keep me from evil, that I may not cause pain!" Would our days be the same if we believed that God wants to increase the territory where we are? Just like the incident with Dixie, if Willa K. were not prepared for a meeting as that turned out to be, what might have happened in this relationship with Dixie? Even though it seems to us that nothing was accomplished in Dixie's life, God knows. God moves in the lives of His people and as stated in the scripture, God's ways are not our ways. He knows the beginning and the ending, even in Dixie's life.

Oodles Of Noodles

I have my family for dinner every Sunday. This particular Sunday I had decided on chicken and noodles over mashed potatoes, a real favorite of the kids! I usually buy canned chicken, but this time I felt extra domesticated so I decided to cook my own chicken. After all, Amy would be here and Toby had been dating her long enough that I wanted to impress her with "homemade" food! I don't know how to make noodles from scratch, so I settled on a pound bag of the good kluski kind.

Sunday came and I made real mashed potatoes instead of the ones from a box, as I normally would have. (Boxed potatoes would be the favorite of the boys!) The family came and we sat around the dining room table enjoying our lunch and the fellowship. I even caught Toby snitching chicken and noodles right out of the serving dish when the meal was over.

Following the meal, the whole gang settled into the living room to watch the weekly NASCAR race, and I began to put leftovers in containers. As I was scraping the bowl containing the chicken and noodles, something caught my eye. As I picked it out, it appeared to be a ring. I quickly washed it and couldn't believe what I saw. It wasn't just a ring; it was a diamond ring! I ran into the living room excitedly and said, "Look at this!" At first I was half ticked at Toby. I thought he might have put Amy's engagement ring in the noodles. How tacky! He couldn't believe I would even think that. We all had a good laugh over it. However, that still didn't change the fact that I had a diamond ring.

All kinds of thoughts went through my mind. Maybe this was a contest or maybe someone had lost it. I went through my wastebasket to find the plastic bag the noodles had come in. The only thing I found was the distributor's address and phone number and was surprised to discover that it was located just thirty miles from us. I put the diamond back into the plastic bag and put it in my purse to take to work. Being Sunday, I knew I would have to wait until the next day to solve this mystery!

When I got to the office Monday morning, I couldn't wait to show the girls. After I relayed the whole story to them, I called the number on the package. The phone rang a couple of times when a gentleman answered. I later found out he was the owner and answered because the employees had the day off since the 4th of July was the next day. I told him I found something in the noodles and his exact words were, "You found it!" He told me that a young lady had lost her diamond ring while packaging noodles. (They since have to take off rings while working!) When she discovered that her ring was missing, they reopened 900 cases (10,800 packages) of noodles searching for her lost diamond ring.

Two days later the young couple came into the office and asked for me. The girl burst into tears at the sight of her ring. They explained how they have been married just two years and were heartsick over losing the ring. They are both employed at the noodle factory. He makes the noodles and she packages them. Her husband showed me his wedding band so that I could see that the etching matched. I cannot tell you how many times they thanked me.

The young couple was shocked at the effort I made to find the ring's owner. They were certain that the finder would keep it or pawn it for money. I know how precious my engagement ring is to me so it never crossed my mind to do anything but try to find the owner. In gratitude the owner sent two cases of noodles, oodles of noodles!

By the way, Toby gave Amy her diamond engagement ring just a few days later in a more traditional way!

Afterthought ... Remember the old saying, "finders-keepers"? What a treasure was found in the lunch of noodles that Sunday. For this young couple it was a symbol of the undying love they had pledged to each other. For Willa K. it was the excitement of finding a hidden treasure. Seeing the faces of this couple as they came to pick up their beautiful ring reminded Willa K. of the importance of her diamond ring and the love she shared with her husband, Lee. Just the fact that the couple thought Willa K. might pawn it or keep it for her own gives us insight to the way the world sees today. May we have a heart like Jesus that just keeps giving and giving and not have a "finders-keepers' heart."

My Leisure Prayer Life

Do you ever have trouble focusing when you pray? If you're like me, sometimes that can be very difficult. I remember this time when Nancy and Amos and Lee and I went to an installation service for a pastor friend and his wife.

When I go to special occasions like that, I take two or three outfits so I have just the right one to wear. When it was time for the service, it was warmer than I had anticipated so I took out my back-up dress, which is something I bought from the leisure section of the store. That means I purchased it in the nightwear department. I had worn the dress many times and no one had ever said, "That looks just like a nightgown!" I thought it was very pretty and so did Nancy.

When we arrived at the church, we were ushered to the very front row. Near the end of the service, the guest speaker said, "Now we're going to have a season of prayer." He started calling people to the front of the church to pray. First he called for the church board. Next he called for the members of the pastoral search committee. And then, to our surprise, he said, "You dear friends on the front row, won't you come and join us too?"

I was thinking, "What, me in my leisure dress?" But we walked to the platform and went up the steps.

Then he said, "Let's kneel." I was a little leery about that one, but I got down on my knees the best I could and we began to pray.

I was okay during the first three prayers. After that, my knees were so numb that I couldn't move. Worse yet, I began to panic about how I was going to get up. Was I worried about anybody praying about anything? No! I was worried about how I was going to get off that platform when everyone else was done praying.

I looked over at Nancy and there she was praying her heart out. She seemed fine. I thought, "Aren't her knees giving out too?" Everyone around me seemed to be doing fine but not me. I thought, "It just must be the position I'm in." I tried to get into a better position. Then I started thinking, isn't anyone ever going to say, "Amen"?

Finally someone said, "Amen," and I looked over at my husband and whispered, "I don't know how I'm going to get off this platform." I just could not move.

In his own quiet way, he leaned over to me and said, "Try scooting backwards." I tried to scoot backwards on my knees until I got to the edge. However, another problem quickly developed. I had a rather deep "v" neckline on my leisure dress and it was getting deeper with each scoot backward! Here's this "v" that became a real "v," a dramatic "v," in the front of my dress.

Lee looked over at me and I could see on his face something was drastically wrong! He said, "COVER IT UP with your hands!" But by that time you could see more than you wanted to see. I tried to cover it with my hand while I got to the edge where I could put my feet down.

When I finally got back to the seat, my husband leaned over and said, "Did you get it covered?"

Almost in tears, I said, "I'm trying, I'm trying."

As I sat there, I thought about how much this was like my prayer life at the time. I would start out with good intentions, but then I would think about something else. Sometimes I wonder how disappointed God must have been when I couldn't keep my mind focused on Him.

Even to this day, I still have a problem keeping my mind focused when I pray. I find that if I sit in the same chair about the same time each day it does get better. Another suggestion, pray out loud.

I can say that there is hope for those whose minds go everywhere but to heaven when you try to pray. Besides, posture doesn't mean that much. It's how we focus with our hearts as we approach God in prayer that is important.

Afterthought ... We can experience a dynamic devotion to the Savior in our life when we focus on devotion as a matter of the heart. Developing an intimate relationship with the living God gives us whole-hearted devotion. Practice patience in prayer. You need to make prayer a habit and a step of obedience everyday. Finding time that is convenient for your lifestyle is not always an easy task to accomplish. Whether it is getting up every day a few minutes earlier than the family begins the day or staying up later than your normal bedtime, finding the time to spend with God is one of the most important steps of obedience you will make. You will find your life will change, you will change, and circumstances around you will change when you make a commitment to a constant prayer life. Prayer changes things and people!

Standing On The Edge
Part 1 — The Past

Standing on the edge I ask you this question, "Are you ready for the harvest?" The harvest is ready. I believe that people today are searching. They're searching for everything, everywhere. But they don't know what they're searching for.

We have the answer they're looking for and need. We are standing on the edge in our lives today. We can look to the past; we can stay in the present, or we can look to the future.

When we look back into our past, some of us think that life was great. We didn't have any kids then. The money was good. We just lived and did what we wanted to do. It was fun. Maybe your health was good. You, Willa K., and I are getting older. Health problems are starting to pop up.

Maybe the past wasn't so good. Maybe there was abuse and hurt. Perhaps there is anger deep inside of you. Maybe there are feelings that are hard for you to overcome. I think about when Amos and I were first married. I didn't grow up in a Christian home. My parents were not Christians, so I rarely attended church. I never had any spiritual training, and I didn't know how to go to the Word to find answers for my problems.

There was a church on the corner close to our home and the pastor, Rev. Lon Calloway, and his family, lived right behind us. They had a daughter, Sharon, who was my age, and we became very good friends. I came to Christ through their witness and testimony. I started going to church and it didn't take very long for me to find that what I was searching for was in God.

Amos and I married, but I had fallen away from the Lord. At that time my husband didn't know the Lord. We moved to Berne, where we live now, but we didn't know anyone. I got pregnant right away. We were so happy and excited. Having a family was all I ever wanted when I was growing up. I thought about being a teacher and that's what my dad would have like for me to be, but I just wanted to get married, have a family, and be at home. That's all I ever desired in my heart. That's why we were so happy when we found out that we were going to have a baby.

Dennis Howard was born a year and a week after our marriage, on November 25, 1963. Oh, what a precious baby. He had a healthy birth weight, and he was so beautiful. He was our dream come true, and everything seemed so perfect in our lives. We took him home from the hospital, and my mother was there to help us for a few weeks. Eight days later he got very sick one morning. He went into convulsions and the doctor said that we needed to get him to the hospital right away. Even from the very beginning we knew that Dennis wasn't going to live. Doctors didn't know what was wrong, but there were a lot of tests they couldn't do on him because he was a newborn.

I remember the morning when the doctor came to us and said, "You're going to have to make a decision about Dennis today. He's on life support, and he hasn't taken a breath on his own since he went on the respirator. The respirator is putting life there that just isn't there anymore."

That was one of the biggest decisions Amos and I have ever had to make. To know that this decision could take the life of the child we had wanted so badly and cherished so much was almost more than we could imagine.

I can remember standing at the bedside of our precious little baby. At that time life support was not automatic. Student nurses had to stand at the machine and take turns turning the switch that gave our baby life. I will never forget hearing the sound of voices counting, "1, 2, 3, 1, 2, 3," as they gave him life. Knowing that my heart wasn't right with God, I prayed to God, "If you take him, I will understand. I know that you are not doing this to hurt me. I know that you are doing this to bring me back to you. Not my will but your will be done."

Still, it was a very difficult time for us when Dennis Howard went to be with Jesus.

Life went on for us, and we had two more dear children, Jennifer and Bob. We claimed the verse in Jeremiah 29:11, "For I know the plans I have for you, declares the Lord, plans to prosper you and not to harm you, plans to give you hope and a future."

God is searching us out and wanting us to come to Him. He didn't just put us here on earth for no apparent reason. Is life passing you by? Are you standing on the edge and looking back? Are you at the same place in your Christian experience you were five, ten, or fifteen years ago?

Can you say, five years ago I was there; today I am here?

I love to listen to young Christians. I remember what it was like when I was excited about His Word as a young Christian. I would just devour it. I couldn't get enough of it. Are we still listening to God; that still, small voice that's inside of us?

Listen to the words in Psalm 46:

> *"God is our refuge and strength, an ever-present help in trouble. Therefore, we will not fear, though the earth give way and the mountains fall into the heart of the sea, though its waters roar and foam and the mountains quake with their surging.*
>
> *There is a river whose streams make glad the city of God, the holy place where the Most High dwells. God is within her, she will not fall; God will help her at break of day. Nations are in an uproar, kingdoms fall; he lifts his voice, the earth melts.*
>
> *The Lord Almighty is with us, the God of Jacob is our fortress. Come and see the works of the Lord, the desolations he has brought on the earth. He makes wars cease to the ends of the earth; he breaks the bow and shatters the spear, he burns the shields with fire.*
>
> *Be still and know that I am God; I will be exalted among the nations, I will be exalted in the earth. The Lord Almighty is with us, the God of Jacob is our fortress."*

How comforting to read scriptures that God wrote years ago, when our hearts have been broken, knowing that we would stand on them for the foundation of our faith today. Looking back and seeing how God has brought us through, and how He has been there for us as we stand on the edge and look back. When we really see how He has been with us, it gives us more strength to look into the present.

Standing On The Edge
Part 11 — The Present

There are times when we look back at the past and the way it used to be thirty years ago. We say, "That was great." However, that doesn't really matter now. The important thing is what we're doing to reach out and help in the present. Are we praying for the younger women and trying to help them? We're supposed to be doing things to help in the present.

I remember a story about the turkey pan. Grandma just made the best turkey you ever tasted. Here's her granddaughter, Susie, and she wanted to have Thanksgiving dinner at her house that year. However, she lived in California and Grandma lived in Florida. There was no way that she could get Grandma's turkey pan.

She called her mom and asked her to call Granny to see if she would ship that pan to her for Thanksgiving. Her mother called Grandma and asked her about the pan.

She said, "That pan always made the best turkeys."

All of a sudden Grandma began to laugh as she said, "It's not the pan that makes the turkey good when you use it. I only used that pan because it's the only one that fit in my oven."

It's not the way we repeat and do things that makes it good. It's we who make things come out the way that they do. There's always a plan as to why things are as they are. We need to be flexible and willing to move on and that is not easy. Are you afraid of what's going to happen if you move on from the past? Don't let Satan make you think you cannot be used by God; always be ready.

There is a woman close to us who had been married for eighteen years. We had been concerned that there might be a problem, but we weren't sure what it was. She was a very quiet woman and never talked much about her problems. After telling her husband things had to change and giving him the opportunity to make the changes, which he did not do, she left. We discovered that she had been under a severe amount of abuse. We couldn't believe what we saw and heard. She had been living in a house without hot

75

water with her two teenage children. She had kept all of this inside of her over the years. No one knew that something like this was going on. She had finally come to grips with the past and knew that she had to move on with her life for the sake of her children.

It is important to remember that when God leads us, He will be there to bless things even when we have to make the most difficult decisions. Don't let fears and doubts keep you from moving on. Don't be afraid of the Lord's hand. Venture out and allow God to work in your life. Go from the past of hurt into the present and future that God has for you.

Philippians 4:8 tells us to think these things: "Whatever is true, whatever is noble, whatever is right, whatever is pure, whatever is lovely, whatever is admirable, if anything is excellent or praiseworthy, think about such things. Whatever you have learned or received or heard from me put into practice. And the God of peace will go with you."

I teach third grade children in a Sunday school class. I tell them to read their Bible and talk to God every day; even if it's only one verse. I encourage them to talk to Him, even if it's asking Him to help with a spelling test that day. Because I know that once you instill those kinds of habits into a young life they won't forget where to go when tough times come. Believe me, they will come! You will need the Word to stand on and the Lord to lean on as you go through difficult times.

During the hard times, I have drawn a lot of strength from God's promise in Romans 8:28: "And we know that in all things God works for the good of those who love him, who have been called according to His purpose." Further down in the chapter He promises us that: "In all things we are move than conquerors through him who loved us."

"For I am convinced that neither death nor life, neither angels nor demons, neither the present or the future, nor any powers, neither height nor depth, nor anything else in all creation, will be able to separate us from the love of God that is in Christ Jesus our Lord."

Don't stay in the past. The important thing to remember is that nothing can separate us from Christ, wherever we are. He'll be with us in the present, past and lead us to the way that is best for us in the future. With His help, we can look forward to the future.

76

Standing On The Edge
Part III — The Future

The older we get, the more we realize how precious life is. Romans 8:28 carried me through the difficult times and God's Word was all that I had to stand on. I knew that God had a purpose for my life and I was doing all that I could to find that purpose and live for Him.

Later in Romans 8, he tells us that we cannot be separated from the love of Christ. He promises that He will hold us up, even through the most difficult times in life. The longer we live, the more we realize that He takes care of us on a daily basis. As we learn to lean on Him, the blessings always come.

Still there are times when it's easy to stand on the edge and look down. Trials come and our hearts are broken; life is hard at those times. There are times when we may not care if we live or die. I know what that feeling is like. I've been there!

Four months after our first baby died, the apartment we lived in burned. The devastating fire destroyed almost one block of downtown Berne. Everything we owned was gone; clothing, including our wedding gifts, pictures, everything! All that we had left was the clothing on our backs and our love for each other.

I'll never forget that day. It was a Palm Sunday, but it was cold and blowing, almost blizzard-like conditions. I had a spring outfit on that day that I just made the week before. They called my husband from the church and told him what was happening. One of our dear friends, Tim Sprunger, drove him to our apartment. Amos tried to run up the stairs, but he was overcome by all the smoke, and he went into shock. Our family doctor, Dr. Luginbill, came and checked on him daily that week as his body was unable to cope with this tragedy.

One of our memories of this time was of a co-worker and church friend, Rufus Amstutz. The evening of the fire he came to where we were staying and brought Amos a complete outfit of clothes (shoes, socks, underwear, pants, shirt, and jacket) to wear to work the next day, even though he was unable to work that week. Our church family surrounded us with love by providing food, shelter, clothes, and furniture; everything to start up housekeeping again within a week after the fire. Isn't that amazing? What love!

On February 7, 1972, our last child was born, John Wesley, what a precious baby! They said he was the most beautiful baby, but his lungs were not developed and he died about 24 hours after his birth. I never got to see him.

I was so bitter. I cried out to God, "Why? Why? Why?" With our first son, Dennis, I could understand that you did it to save me, but now John Wesley; why him?

Amos and I were so active in the church, attending services with our children and serving where we were needed. We felt we were where God wanted us to be for that time. I couldn't understand why God would do this when it was all I wanted. I thought of all the people who had baby after baby and didn't take care of them, or hurt them and abused them. It was on my heart day and night.

I wanted to give up. It didn't matter that God had already given us two beautiful and healthy children. I had Jennifer and Bob. I was still angry with God even though I knew that He always loved me no matter what.

I remember one night when some of our friends came over to the house. I was on the sofa where I spent much of my time during those days. They had a young son about the age of our daughter. I was crying and I could hear their son, Dean, saying, "What's wrong with Nancy? Why is she crying?"

His parents tried to take him out of the room, and I could hear them explaining to him about what had happened. Then I heard him say, "But doesn't she know that he's up in heaven with Jesus now?"

Well, I did know that, but that's not what I wanted to hear. I wanted him down here on earth with me. I can remember that Amos and the kids went off to a ball game with our friends that evening. I was praying and asking God, "Why?" All of a sudden the Holy Spirit enclosed the four walls of that room so that the Lord could speak to me. I remember in the quietness and amidst of all the bitterness that was inside of me, God spoke. His words were the beautiful and familiar verse: "Blessed are those who mourn, for they shall be comforted." [Matthew 5:4]

I'd like to say that immediately I was better. My Heavenly Father comforted me and in time my bitterness was overcome by His love. Today I can say I don't feel the same way that I did then. Now when I think of heaven and what awaits me there, my heart has a longing to be there. After all, John Wesley will be there; Dennis Howard will be there, and most of all, Jesus will be there.

Have you ever seen stagnant water? It's awful, isn't it? It smells bad and it looks bad. No one wants to be around it, either. Sometimes our lives can be like that. We need to keep moving on with what God has for us. We can't dwell on the past, or even get stagnant in the present. We need to keep looking ahead and trusting God to lead our way.

Standing on the edge isn't the place God wants us to be, so don't be afraid to move forward. Are you ready for the future? God has something for you.

Do you remember how we used to play hide and go seek? Remember those words, "One, two, three — here I come, ready or not"? God doesn't hide from us like that. He waits for us with open arms. He died on the cross for us with His arms open wide ready to receive us.

God will meet us at any time in our lives. Whether we are younger or older. Stretch forth your hands and get ready to go with the Father. He'll give you new hope, a new way of life, and new opportunities. The Bible says that Jesus Christ is the same, yesterday, today, and forever — past, present, and future — He'll meet us at the edge and lead us to safety in Him.

Sidney Marie

Sidney Marie is the joy of my life. She's my three-year-old granddaughter, and she just says the most wonderful things to her grandma. She comes running over to me and says, "Oh, Grandma, I love you." Then she puts her arms around me and I can't tell you what that means to me.

Some people say that a grandma is a grandma is a grandma. I'm really a grandma. It seems like grandkids are much more fun than kids ever were. Nancy always told me it would be that way, but I never believed her!

We were celebrating Amy's birthday and had decided on Cheddars. As we were waiting in line for a table, out came those famous words, "I have to go potty." So I volunteered to take her and we waited in line outside the restroom. Finally we made it inside the door only to wait in another line. It was so cute, she waited like a little lady and finally it was her turn. After she finished, I said, "Honey, can you wait for Grandma to go potty?" She assured me that she could, but I wasn't prepared for what was going to come next. My little granddaughter looked at me with her big eyes and blurted out loudly, "Grandma, you REALLY have a big belly!"

I could just hear the snickers of everyone outside and knew everyone would be watching when we exited the stall. So, when we came out I said, "Yes, I'm the grandma with the big belly!" It was so funny! You should have seen the people. They all looked around as if to say, "We don't know what she's talking about. Did somebody say something?"

Another time my husband and I had taken her out to Hardees. She had finished her meal and we had just washed her hands. She had one chicken nugget left and I asked her, "Sidney, can Grandpa eat your last chicken nugget?"

"He can have it," she replied.

My husband ate the chicken nugget and all of a sudden she put her hands on her cheeks and cried out, "My grandpa ate ALL MY FOOD!"

My husband and I are big people and everybody looked as if to say, "What kind of a family is this that would eat this dear, sweet child's food?" About all you can do at a moment like that is take her up in your arms and carry her out of the restaurant, hoping that no one knows who you are. Ironically, we have never been back to that Hardees with her!

One evening I was talking to Jeff and he told me that Sidney said she knew that she had to wash her hands because her mom always makes her wash her hands. Then she said, "Grandma Charlie always makes me wash my hands, but the 'other grandma' doesn't."

Wouldn't you know, I'm the "other grandma"!

But in spite of what Sidney says we just love her so much. There's nothing she could say that would ever change that. She's our grandchild and we just love her so much in spite of what she says or does. Her hugs, her honesty, all that she is brings joy to our life.

Afterthought ... When we think of our love for Sidney, we are reminded that the Heavenly Father loves us even more. We know that we make mistakes and say things that are out of line; and yet, He loves us with unconditional love.

Do you know what? I just absolutely adore Sidney. It doesn't matter what she says, I still love her, and that's the way Jesus loves you and me. I John 3:1 says that God has lavished His love on us in that we should be called the children of God. No matter what you have done or what you say, He loves you. Run to Him and He'll put His arms around you and lift you up as His child that He adores.

82

The Circling Boat

One of the most important areas of my life is my friends. Nancy is my very best friend. Sometimes I think the reason we are best friends is because we are the complete opposite. If I had my "druthers" I would go before audiences in blue jeans and a T-shirt. Nancy is always dressed up. We argue about how to raise our children. She raises hers and I raise mine, but we don't agree about it. There's nothing we could say that could make a difference.

We even vacation together. Every year we go to Lake Wawasee in northern Indiana and rent cottages at Oakwood Park. Our kids used to play together, but now they're too old for that, so they just play golf together. I remember this particular time when we had just arrived. As we were starting to unload things I heard sirens. I remember thinking, "I'm so glad we're all accounted for." When you know that your children are out on the road and you hear sirens, you always think, "I hope they're okay." But this time I knew that we were all together at the lake and everything was okay, or at least so I thought.

I was in the kitchen when Lee came in and said, "Honey, the boys' boat is in the middle of the lake, and it's going around and around. But they say Aaron is okay."

Right away I thought, "How could a man get a story so messed up?" I was half upset with him for telling me a story I knew couldn't be true. After all, how could a boat be going around in circles in the middle of a lake with no one in it?

We ran out the front door and down to the pier, and sure enough, there it was. I could see the boys' black boat going around and around in circles with nobody in it. Right away I froze. What happened? Where was Aaron? Was he all right?

My husband said, "He's all right. Honestly, he's all right!"

But that wasn't good enough. I wanted to see him. I wanted to know that he was okay. No one's assurances made any difference at that point until I could see for myself that he was okay. Desperate, I ran into the hotel lobby and started crying for help only to have a dear, sweet elderly lady tell me she didn't know what to do either! How was I to know she was only a volunteer in the candy store? Someone had to show me that my son was okay.

In the meantime, Jeff and Tami had gotten on their bikes and rode to Wurster's cottage, friends from our hometown. Jeff told them what had happened and they got in their boat and went out to the circling boat. There they found Aaron, who had been picked up by another boat that had gone out to rescue him. Aaron got into Wurster's boat and headed for shore. By then I was back on the pier frantic and desperately wanting to know something about Aaron. At first they weren't going to let the boat come close because of shoreline regulations. Finally, when one of the authorities realized I wouldn't calm down, he said, "Let her see that boy." They allowed the boat to come to the pier and I could see Aaron.

I cried, "Aaron, how are you? Are you okay?"

He replied, "Mom, I'm okay. I don't know what happened. A wave came and suddenly I was out of the boat."

In the meantime, that boat was still out there in the water just going around and around. The police came and said, "How much gas do you have in there?"

Jeff replied, "I just filled it up."

They said, "Well, we can't let it run out of gas."

I couldn't believe how much attention this whole situation had attracted. I looked out toward the boat and there were all of these flashing lights. On one pier was the fire department. On another was the EMS. On another was the police, all because of our boat. There was even talk of dropping someone down by helicopter to try to shut the boat off. I began to realize just how serious this situation was. It dawned on me that someone could get hurt trying to rescue our boat.

Just then, out of nowhere, two young men on jet skis came riding up to the Department of Natural Resources men who were in charge of the incident and said, "We could ride in to the circle and jump into the boat and shut it off."

That sounded pretty good to me, but the DNR officer said, "You're not going to do that. It's too dangerous."

They looked at him and suddenly took off. They rode their jet skis right into the middle of the circle and tried to jump into the boat, but they missed. Our hearts sank, fearful for the young men and for what the boat could do if it didn't continue to go around and around. They tried again and this time it worked, and they turned off the motor. They immediately rode off into the channel because they were afraid they were going to get in trouble. We never were able to find out who those young men were, but we were very grateful for what they had done.

Later that night Aaron took the boat for a ride. We encouraged him to not be afraid because of what had happened. It was just one of those things that happen.

A few years later when Aaron was attending Taylor University, he was telling this story one day. All of a sudden one of the students said, "Was that you? We heard all about it."

Aaron said, "Do you know who the guys were on the jet skis? They took off because they didn't want to get into trouble."

The student replied, "We don't have any idea who they were."

"If anybody knows who they are," said Aaron, "I just want to thank them for what they did that day."

Afterthought ... The anxious heart that Lee and Willa K. experienced the day of the boat accident was almost more than they could conceive. Not knowing if their son, their baby, was in the boat, or in the middle of the circle was agony they had never experienced before. They were confused and distraught. Where was their son? They needed to know that Aaron was okay! Even when they were told that Aaron was in another boat, they needed assurance he was in another boat! Just being told was not good enough! Only when they could see him and touch him were they convinced that their son was okay.

It is the same with some of us today. We cannot believe that Jesus has saved us. Our faith is so weak we falter in belief. Hebrews tells us that without faith we cannot please God. Do we want to please God? Of course we do. If you have prayed the prayer of confession and believed on the Lord Jesus Christ as your Savior, you will want to live for Him. We cannot live for Him if we do not believe Him. It is so simple; the Bible says even a little child can understand the love of God. His love is unconditional! We will fail, we will make mistakes, and we will falter, but at those times just release yourself to the Father and let His will be done in your life.

Lee and Willa K. were so anxious during those minutes at the lake. I know they would say today that in times like that is when you draw upon that hidden strength, "your belief," that comes from God.

The Gravy Trail

Lee and I were married only two weeks when I decided to make gravy for the first time. I had watched my mom make it hundreds of times, no problem!

I fried the meat, took it out of the skillet and began to make the gravy. I put some flour in, then added some water, a little more flour. When Lee saw what I was doing and said, "My mom always uses milk to make her gravy," I added some milk to make him happy. After all, we were only married two weeks!

I continued to stir, adding a little more flour, a little more water (excuse me, milk) until I had a skillet full of something that looked gross with the consistency of goop! I knew then that it was a lost cause and decided to chuck the idea of gravy for supper that night and talk to Mom about my failure. I put the "gravy" in an old glass mayonnaise jar and put it under the sink until trash day.

The next day I took the jar, along with some other trash, out to the garbage can. It was a cold day and the jar slipped from my hands, falling to the cement floor. The jar broke, however, my gravy STOOD! I cleaned up the mess and headed over to Mom's to find out what I did wrong.

She said, "I'm so sorry. I think I know what went wrong. You have new pans and you need to have seasoned ones, so take my pan and the next time, don't use so much flour. You can do it, it's easy!"

A couple of days later I tried again and it went wonderfully well. It looked really great, but did not taste as good as Mom's, but, I thought, "It's close!"

So you can imagine my joy when I put the mashed potatoes and gravy in front of Lee that night for supper. I could hardly wait to see the expression on his face when he tasted my delicious gravy! He took one bite. I looked for the approval on his face, but it never came. I began to cry and quickly Lee said, "Please don't cry ... I've had worse!"

I sobbed, "Where?"

He said slowly, "The army!"

I was devastated but confident I could make it better the next time.

The next time I fried meat, I ran next door to my mom's house, and she made the gravy. Then I would go back home, Lee would come home, and we would have the best gravy in the world! He would tell me so!

We kept this up for a few years until my folks moved to Swiss Village, a retirement community. Since then, we have not had gravy at our home unless it is over a roast and made with soup! I fix a lot of things but you will never have gravy at my home. Actually, I have had it when company has come but only when Nancy is invited so she can make the gravy.

Afterthought ... Who's a cook out there? Many of you, I'm sure. Willa K. and I love to cook. As a matter of fact we had a catering business together for several years. Now we just enjoy cooking for our families and especially our Monday night Bible study. We each have different cooking talents. Willa is much more frugal than I. It doesn't bother her to use every little leftover in the refrigerator and blend a casserole that brings delight to all she serves. I, on the other hand, am a meat and potatoes cook. Even though we work well in the kitchen together, we each have our own corner.

Isn't life that way? We all have gifts and talents given by the Master. What a shame when they lie dormant. What a disappointment to God. If we decide we will never try again after a few failures, we are not giving God the time He deserves to develop them in us. Today meditate on those things God wants to develop in your life, and give Him time!

My Little Black Flats

It was one of those typical winter days, when we had a surprise snowstorm! I was not prepared for it and I didn't even have a pair of boots with me. We decided to close the office early so all the employees could get home in the daylight, so I offered to get the deposit ready, lock the doors, and be the last to leave as I lived the closest to the office. Before I left I called the local pizza parlor and ordered one for takeout, as I didn't feel like fixing supper that night.

When I got to my van I was pleasantly surprised that someone had brushed the deep snow off of it and all I had to do was get in and go! I was grateful as I had my black flats on and they were not the ideal shoes in snow!

I drove to the local bank where I got in line to give them the deposit. I was the third car in line when it dawned on me that I should check my power window. Sometimes the window will not go down because of the snow and ice that builds up, and sure enough, it didn't work. I decided to do what Lee does when this happens; with one hand you push the power button and with the other you try to gently push the window down. It didn't work! I knew I had to get that window down. It is terribly embarrassing to get to the drive-thru window and then not get it down! So, I chose to get out of the van and try to get the snow out of the window along the bottom. I opened the door, stepped on the running board and slipped, sending me down into the snow! I sat up, looked to see if anyone saw me, and got up as fast as I could in the ice-covered snow! Thank goodness, I was in the right drive-thru window and everyone was on the other side of the van! Whoa! I was lucky! No one saw! I was going to get back into the van but noticed something was wrong. I was missing a shoe, my black flat! I looked around and could not find it. Now I would have just gotten into the van and forgotten the old shoe, but I couldn't get the pizza without shoes on! No shirt, no shoes, no service policy! And, it would look bad with only one shoe on with businesses closing because of so-o-o-o much snow! So, I knew it had to be under the van. I got down on my stomach, looked under the van, and there it was. I tried to get it but it was out of reach. In desperation I took my other shoe off and tried to swat it and there it went, in front of the van. I got up, brushed the snow off again, and, as stately as I could, walked in front of the van and picked up the shoe! I did not look around, clinging to the hope that no one saw me!

I got back into the van and moved up another car length, and soon it was my turn. By that time my power window was working, so I smiled at the teller and said, "Hi, how are you?"

"Fine," she said, "And you?"

"Just great," I replied, sitting there in wet feet and snow all over my coat! "Thanks," I said as I pulled away from the window!

"Boy, I pulled that off," I thought to myself as I went to pick up the pizza and then home! I told Lee about my adventure and said, "Can you believe it?"

He said very matter-of-factly, "Yes."

A few days later I went to the branch bank and went inside to do my transaction. As I was standing in line I saw something I had never seen before. Up in the corner of the bank appeared to be a little TV set with cars on the picture. I asked the teller, "Where is that coming from?"

She cried out, "Was that YOU?"

Knowing full well she had seen the video of me that snowy day, I said to her, "What do you mean?"

She regained her composure and said, "O-o-oh, I'm sorry; it's nothing."

I left and never did admit to anyone I knew they knew it was I that snowy day!

Now I know you are all wondering about the video. It is my understanding that it cannot be sent to *America's Funniest Videos* without my permission, and they will *never* get it!

Afterthought ... How many of you believe this could only happen to Willa K.? I would tend to believe this but know of those kinds of predicaments I have been in myself. And that's all I'll say about that!

Are there times in your life when you wouldn't want the eye of a camera recording your doings? Probably in all of our lives there are times we could say, "Don't put the camera on me!" The last three years Jesus walked on earth the eye of the camera was on Him. We have a living record, in our Bibles, of his life. What an example He left for us to follow.

In I Corinthians 4:5 we read: "Therefore judge nothing before the time, until the Lord comes, who will both bring to light the hidden things of darkness and reveal the counsels of the hearts. Then each one's praise will come from God." We are expected to be found faithful.

And The Winner Is!

We had been looking at purchasing a truck. Lee had gone to a dealer when he learned of a contest featuring a truck give-away. He consented to have his name stand in the pool of names for drawings related to the give-away. He also learned that certain names would be drawn during the 6:00 news of a local television station. The station had a number you were supposed to call within fifteen minutes to win the truck.

A few nights later I was visiting with Nancy and she happened to have the news program on her television. All of a sudden there was a break and they flashed a name over the screen. It read, "Leland Sprunger, Berne, Indiana."

"Oh, oh, oh my," I said to Nancy. "This is the greatest thing that's ever happened. This is the most wonderful thing. I have to find Lee. He's at school. We've only got fifteen minutes to call."

I literally ran to the van and took off for the school. But wouldn't you know I hit the only red light in our town and I sat there and waited for what seemed like an eternity. Actually it was only one minute!

"I've already used up two minutes of my time," I thought to myself. And I can't go right to the school. I have to get the number. I have to go to the house and get the number. Oh dear, where is that number? I have to hurry.

I pulled up in front of the house and ran in. By that time, I was out of breath, and it felt like my heart was beating in my throat! "I have to hurry," I thought. "I'm losing precious moments." I found the number and headed over to the school; thank goodness it's only a half a block away.

The next problem would be finding a door that was open. I went to the first door and it was locked. I tried the second door and it wouldn't open, either. Finally, I found one that opened and I ran into the school screaming, "Lee, Lee, Lee."

By that time he came running because he thought there was something drastically wrong.

He said, "What's wrong?"

I said, "The number, the number; you have to call the number."

He was far less excited than I was, but he looked at me and said, "What number, what number am I supposed to call?"

By that time I was so excited I could hardly talk, and I said, "The truck, you know, the truck that they're giving away."

Very nonchalantly he answered, "Oh, that number."

We were on our way to the office phone when someone started hammering the doors. We looked and it was our neighbor lady, Connie.

"Call the number," she yelled from the outside. "Your name was on TV. Call that number."

Just then Jeff came running with a cell phone and yelled, "Dad, call the number; your name; they called your name."

Very calmly in the midst of all of this, Lee called the television station. It was then that we found out that this contest happened in steps. Our name would now be placed in a big hopper where one name would be drawn at the end of the month. That was the person that would get the truck. We had won a T-shirt! Incidentally, Toby received eleven phone calls on the answering machine in a fifteen-minute span letting him know that his Dad's name had been chosen for the drawing.

I went home so disappointed. I don't always know a lot, but I know the difference between a truck and a T-shirt. I thought, "All of that excitement for a T-shirt and a 'chance' to win the truck."

Isn't that amazing? You know, I think that is where many of us are. People around us are hurting; we have the answer, but we don't share it. We have the means to tell people about the peace they can find in Christ, but we don't do anything about it. Isn't that something? We can get so excited about a truck, and we have the answer for peace in the world and in men's hearts, and we can't get excited enough about it to do anything. Tell us that we might win a truck and we go crazy, but why don't we get that excited about telling people about the Lord?

The T-shirt was okay, and the truck would have been great, but there was a lesson I learned from my excitement that evening that is probably more valuable than even a truck. Keep things in perspective and keep my priorities where they should be. Keep my excitement where it should be (in the Lord Jesus Christ) and God will take care of the rest.

Afterthought ... How many of us like to be a winner? Every one of us does. I can even get excited over a game show on television. I have even been known to cry when someone wins the grand prize. I can get excited at a ball game when my team is winning. Afterwards I sometimes think, "I wonder if anyone was watching how ridiculous I was behaving." How about you? Do you get excited at sports events or watching television? I can remember one summer at a swim meet where Willa K.'s son was competing. She was so excited that when the swimming event was over and Jeff had won, she was on top of the table where she was keeping score. She couldn't even remember how she had gotten on top of the table! Now that's getting excited!

When someone comes to the Lord, do we even acknowledge what God has done in a life? Do we sit back and say, "Will he make it or will he fail?" Or do we say, "I will pray for him; I will be an encourager; I will send him a note today!" I trust you will. The Father says that we need each other for love, encouragement, working, and sharing. Let's obey the voice of the Father.

Mother Of The Groom

Aaron and Kathy had been dating almost two years when we heard the great news, "We're getting married!" We were so excited! Being the in-charge type of person I am, my mind was in full swing, planning this and that, wanting this to be the perfect wedding. After all, Aaron was my baby. Then I am reminded that I am the mother of the groom and my job is to dress in something that blends well and to keep my mouth shut! This is very difficult for me to do, but I thought I was doing quite well, thank you! I found this great black dress with a long coat six months before the wedding and purchased it a little small, knowing I would be able to get into it by November.

Well, time passed but the weight didn't, so I tried it on just one week before the wedding! And would you believe this, it was still too tight! My husband was most accommodating when we rearranged our day and headed to the mall thirty miles away. I found another black dress within an hour as the holiday dresses were now on the rack and I was thrilled. I actually had to decide between a few of them so I was pleased with the new gown!

Now, I had been praying that everything would go as planned. But I was also asking God for a sweet spirit, as I am the type of person who has the answer! If anyone asks, or sometimes they don't even ask, I always have an answer! So, I asked God to help me to keep a low profile and remember that this is Kathy's wedding!

Everything was falling into place, as we only had to host the rehearsal dinner; Nancy and Amos were taking care of the details. I got my hair done for the rehearsal and had my first set of fake nails put on just hours before we left for the hotel an hour away. I even stopped at the Wal-Mart to get a nail repair kit so I was prepared for everything.

Meanwhile, I noticed a raspy throat and decided to swing by the doctor's office to see if they could give me anything. The doctor prescribed a couple of medications to help with the problem so I knew I would be better quickly. After all, I didn't feel bad so what could possibly be wrong?

We arrived at the hotel and quickly dressed for the rehearsal. It was an exceptionally warm November evening and I hardly knew what to wear. However, I had bought a velvet pantsuit for this occasion and I was going to wear it even if it was too warm for velvet. We were off to the church, leaving Nancy and Amos with all the rehearsal dinner responsibilities. This was truly going to be a night to enjoy and remember for a lifetime.

I behaved very well at the rehearsal, as my voice kept getting weaker and weaker. When we finally got to the dinner my voice was gone completely! I had planned this great time of sharing things Aaron had written as a child, but it all had to be changed! Nancy was kind enough to take over, but it just wasn't the same. I think Aaron was relieved, but I knew I needed to rest my voice for the wedding the next day.

In the morning my voice was not better. I went to get my hair done again (it takes a lot to make me look good!), but my voice was still gone. It was finally time for the wedding and what a beautiful wedding! I knew it was because all I could do was smile, gesture, and nod, anything but talk! At the reception we were seated at the table with family, and I would have to whisper to Lee so he could relay my conversation to my sister who was sitting across from me.

All of a sudden the light bulb went off in my head! I had prayed that I would have a sweet spirit, and I guess God wasn't going to take any chances with me, so He took my voice completely away! It was very evident to me because, when I woke up at the hotel on Sunday morning, my voice was back! So, be careful what you pray for ... God may give you exactly what you ask!

Afterthought ... Yes, it was a wonderful wedding. All the preparations and love that went into those hours were blessed. God is so good in all He does for His children. It is wonderful to watch Aaron and Kathy grow in their love for each other and in their love for their Lord.

A verse that Willa K. reads in her daily devotions after she prays comes from the psalmist David in chapter 5, verse 3, "Morning by morning, O Lord, you hear my voice; morning by morning

98

I lay my requests before you and wait in expectation." Doesn't God have a sense of humor! He is listening to our every prayer, even when sometimes we feel He is not there. Sometimes we want to be glib or not really thinking about what we are talking to the Lord about. Be assured today that God cares and He is listening to your requests. Wait in expectation on Him!

Dear Reader,

This book was written because of the encouragement from the women we meet with in a Monday night Bible study. For many years we have had a dream to write. We have struggled over the years in indecision as to where we should begin, even after much prayer and waiting on the Lord. One evening while studying a chapter on "wanting to do more" we realized God was ready for us to pursue our dream. Nancy is an avid reader and Willa K. is not a reader at all, so this was not an easy decision.

We are so thankful that God has given us the ministry of encouragement. Over the years we have traveled coast-to-coast, sharing the joy that comes from serving Jesus! We trust that you have caught the excitement in reading the true stories from our lives. It is our prayer that the Lord will use our humor and dedication to Him to put a smile on your face and a commitment in your heart.

After reading this book, if you have prayed the prayer of salvation, or you have been encouraged and uplifted, we would love to hear from you. Please write and tell us your experience and send it to one of the addresses below.

Willa K. Sprunger
756 W. Water St.
Berne, IN 46711

Nancy G. Lindsey
806 E. Water St.
Berne, IN 46711

To order copies of this book, please send $12.00 to

756 W. Water St.
Berne, IN 46711

Allow three weeks for delivery.